Listening To God

CHARLES
STANLEY

THOMAS NELSON PUBLISHERS
Nashville • Atlanta • London • Vancouver

Published in Nashville, Tennessee, by Thomas Nelson, Inc., Publishers, and distributed in Canada by Word Communications, Ltd., Richmond, British Columbia.

ISBN 0-7852-7257-7

Printed in the United States of America.

5 6 — 01 00 99 98 97

Contents

INTRODUCTION

God Has Something to Say to You

One of the most important lessons in life that you and I can learn is how to listen to God. In our complex and hectic lives, nothing is more urgent, nothing more necessary, and nothing more rewarding than hearing what God has to say to us—both as bodies of believers and as individual people.

If you are going to develop a relationship with another person, you have to converse with that person in some manner. That means both talking and listening. Most of us do better with the talking part. In my ministry, there was a time when I was too occupied doing the Lord's work to pay close attention to God's voice. I was preaching six times a week, taping two television programs, traveling across the nation, writing a book, pastoring the church, and administrating a large church staff and broadcast ministry (among other daily duties). In the midst of it all, I spent time talking to God, very often about the needs that I was facing in my personal life and ministry, but not much time listening to God. I ended up in the hospital for a week and out of circulation for three months. The net result for all of us if we don't learn how to listen to God is that we can make unwise and, ultimately, very costly mistakes.

You may ask, "Does God really speak to us today?" The Bible assures us that He does. The book of Hebrews opens this way: "God, who at various times and in various ways spoke in time past to the fathers by the prophets, has in these last days spoken to us by His Son, whom He has appointed heir of all things, through whom also He made the worlds" (Heb. 1:1–2).

Our God is not a speechless God. Our God is alive and active in our world. He speaks! Furthermore, He doesn't speak to us in veiled terms, riddles, or mysteries. He speaks to us plainly. The goal of any communicator is not to speak well but to be heard. God speaks in a way that we can hear Him, receive His message clearly, and understand with precision what He wants us to do.

A Highly Personal Word

God not only speaks in general and absolute terms to all people, but He speaks to each one of us personally. We can hardly comprehend that possibility with our finite minds. God is an infinite God, and He is capable of communicating with each one of us, right where we are—in the midst of our current circumstances or crises—in very personal, direct, and explicit terms.

This may be the most important concept you can ever grasp in learning how to listen to God. When God speaks, He is speaking to you. Everything in the Bible applies to your life in some way. Every message or communication that is based on the Word of God has truth embedded within it that is for you. There is no such thing as a chapter in the Bible, a sermon based on God's Word, or a book that expounds and explains God's Word that is not for you. Each of us must take God's Word personally!

Personal Does Not Mean Exclusive

This is not to say that God has an exclusive word for a person. God doesn't deal in secrets. He won't reveal truth to one person and deny it to another. Be on guard if you hear somebody say, "God told me something, but He told me I can't tell anybody else," or "God had a word that's just for me and not for you." God doesn't play favorites. He doesn't speak to one child and totally ignore His other children. His word of correction to you may be so personal that you don't want to share it with other people, but ultimately, God's word of correction is an absolute that applies to all people. The same goes for God's promises, provisions, and insights.

Always Important

God doesn't speak frivolously. He doesn't joke around. God means what He says. He will do what He says. God is serious about His relationship with you. He doesn't speak to you in idle terms. He expects you to respond to His voice, heed His Word, and act on it.

Can you remember last Sunday's sermon? Can you recall what you read in God's Word yesterday? You'll be able to remember if you were listening for what God had to say to you and if you take seriously the idea that God intends for you to do something in response to His Word.

God speaks for your benefit. He desires for you to listen to Him and then respond to His words. Sometimes He will challenge you to change your thinking or to release certain feelings and opinions that you have been harboring. Sometimes He will command you to change certain aspects of your behavior. Sometimes He desires to encourage you so that you might live your life with greater joy and strength. Always, however, God's Word is for your transformation. It is intended to change you in some way.

Approach God's Word seriously. Listening to God is not a casual pastime or a let's-try-it-and-see-if-you-like-it activity. Listening to God is the most important thing you can do in your life for your eternal sake.

LESSON 1

PREPARING TO HEAR FROM GOD

This book is for Bible study. As you engage in this study, refer to your Bible again and again—to mark specific words, underline phrases, or write in the margins. I believe God dearly loves to see Bibles that are marked with oil from our fingers, stained with tears from our eyes, and noted with dates and insights.

The Bible is God's foremost method of communication with us today. It is the wellspring from which new insights and eternal wisdom come to us. It is the reference to which we must return continually to check out messages that we believe are from God. I believe it is far more important for you to write what you learn from this study guide into the margins and end pages of your Bible than for you to write passages of the Bible into this book.

Keys to Study

You will be asked at various points to identify with the material presented by answering one or more of these questions:

- What new insight have you gained?
- Have you ever had a similar experience?
- How do you feel about this?
- In what way are you challenged to act?

Insights

An insight is more than a fact or an idea. It is seeing something as if it is new to you. You may have read a particular verse many times. You may have studied it, analyzed it, and meditated on it until you think there is nothing else you can know about it. And then, God has a surprise for you! Suddenly, He reveals new meaning to you. That is a spiritual insight.

Insights are usually very personal—something in a verse or passage stands out to you because it relates to you in some way or applies to what you are experiencing right now in your life.

Ask God to give you insights every time you open His Word to read it. I believe He'll answer that prayer.

I find that noting the insights is important in Bible study. When we are focused on identifying the insights God gives us, we tend to look and listen for them more diligently. And the more we look and listen for insights, the more God gives them to us.

The fact is, if you haven't gained new spiritual insights after reading several passages from God's Word, you haven't truly been engaged in the process of studying. From time to time in this study, you'll be asked to note what specific passages of the Bible say to you.

Experiences

We come to God's Word from unique backgrounds. Therefore, each of us has a unique perspective toward what is read. The person who has been raised in the church from childhood, and who is thoroughly familiar with Bible stories, may have a different understanding of a passage from that of a person who is new in the faith or is a beginner in Bible study. In a group, this difference of familiarity with the Bible can sometimes create problems. People with a long history of regularly reading God's Word may lose patience with beginners, and beginners may feel overwhelmed or lost.

We do have in common, however, our life experiences. We can point to times in which we have found the Bible to be very applicable to our lives, sometimes in a confirming, encouraging way, and sometimes in a convicting, challenging way. We have experiences about which we can say, "I know that truth in the Bible is real because of what happened to me."

Our experiences do not make the Bible true, of course. The Bible is truth, period. Nevertheless, as we share our experiences and how they relate to God's Word, we find that God's Word applies to our lives in more ways than we ever thought. We begin to see how God's Word speaks to each person and to each type of experience or situation that a man or woman will have.

Sharing experiences in your journey of faith is important for your spiritual growth. Even if you are doing this study on your own, I encourage you to converse with others about your faith experiences.

Emotional Response

Just as each of us has unique experiences in life, each of us has unique emotional responses to God's Word. No emotional response is more valid than another. You may be frightened or perplexed by—or feel great joy or relief at—what you read. Another person may have a very different response.

Face your emotions honestly. Learn to share your emotions with others. This does not mean in any way that your emotions give validity to the Scriptures or that you should trust your emotions as being the gauge of your faith. Your faith is based on what God says, not what you feel. At the same time, you need to recognize that the Bible has an emotional impact on you. You cannot read the Word of God with an open heart and mind and not have an emotional response to it. Sometimes you may be moved to tears by what you read; at other times you may feel great elation, conviction, hope, love, longing, surprise, or a host of other emotions.

I am asking you to recognize that the Scriptures allow us to have an emotional response to them. God created us with emotions. He knows that we feel certain ways toward Him, toward others, and toward His Word. When we identify how we feel about what God says to us, we often can begin to overcome the inertia that keeps us from actually living out God's Word in our lives and start doing what God tells us to do—with joy and thanksgiving, and with humbleness of spirit.

For example, if we face up to the fact that we are scared to do something we believe God is asking us to do, and if we begin to explore why we are scared, very often we come to deeper insights into ourselves, and—as we continue to dig into God's Word—we find that God has given us provision and offered us help so that we can work through the fear.

In very few instances have I found it helpful to the strengthening and deepening of my faith to hear a person's opinion about biblical passages. Scholarly commentaries certainly have their place in teaching us the context and background of certain passages. But a person's opinion is of little significance when we study the Bible. It is what God says to us that is truly significant. And God often speaks to us in the language of the heart—the unspoken language of our intuition, our emotions, and our innermost desires and longings. When we share our feelings with one another, we grow closer together as the body of Christ; sharing our opinions with one another rarely creates this type of community or unity of spirit in Christ Jesus.

Challenges

As we read God's Word, we nearly always come to what I call a "gulp point." Something we read challenges us to change something in our lives, to gulp and say, "Wow! That really hit me. I need to do something about that." Sometimes it's a conviction about sin in our lives. Sometimes it's a correction in the way we have been taught or the way in which we act toward others. Sometimes it's a clear call to engage in a new discipline or area of ministry. I know with certainty in my life that God never ceases to challenge me just beyond my ability so that I must always rely upon Him to work in me and through me. God is never content with the status quo—He always wants us to grow more like His Son, Jesus Christ.

I believe we need to pinpoint, as best we can, the areas in which we believe God is challenging us, stretching us, causing us to believe for more. When we say to ourselves, "This is what I believe

God wants me to do next," we are identifying the next step upward to a higher plane in our faith walk. The person who isn't challenged to take a next step upward very likely isn't growing and also isn't going with the gospel into areas where God's Word isn't readily heard or understood.

Ultimately, God desires to get His Word into us, and us into His Word, so we can take His Word into the world, live it out, and be witnesses of His Word in all that we say and do. The truth of what God says to us becomes very real and virtually unforgettable when we do His Word, not merely read or study it. Therefore, it isn't enough to clarify our insights, recall our experiences, or identify our emotions. We must apply what we learn. The Bible challenges us to be doers of His Word and not hearers only (James 1:22).

If you don't have somebody to talk to about your insights, experiences, emotions, and challenges, I encourage you to find somebody. Perhaps you can start a Bible study using this book in your home. Perhaps you can talk to your pastor about organizing Bible study groups in your church. There is much to be learned on your own. There is much more to be learned as you become part of a small group that desires to grow in the Lord.

Keep the Bible Central

You may use the book you hold in your hands as a personal study or as part of a small group study. In either situation, I caution you to keep the Bible at the center of all you do. Don't let a Bible study group turn into a support group. Those types of groups have their time and place, but it is as we gather around God's Word—as if we were gathering around a banquet table for a spiritually nutritious meal—that we truly grow in the Lord and become all that He created and designed us to be.

If you are doing a personal Bible study, you must be diligent in keeping your focus on God's Word. Self-analysis is not the goal of this study. Growing up into the fullness of the stature of Christ Jesus is the goal.

Prayer

Finally, I encourage you to begin and end your Bible study times in prayer. Ask God to give you spiritual eyes to see what He wants you to see and spiritual ears to hear what He wants you to hear. Ask Him to give you new insights, to recall to your memory experiences that relate to what you read, and to help you identify your emotional responses. Ask Him to reveal to you what He desires for you to be, say, and do.

As you conclude your time of study, ask the Lord to seal what you have learned in your heart so that you will never forget it. Ask Him to transform you more into the likeness of Jesus Christ as you meditate on what you have studied. And above all, ask Him to give you the courage to become, say, and do what He has challenged you to become, say, and do!

And now consider these questions:

- *What new insights into listening to God do you hope to gain from this study?*

  ____

  ____

- *In what areas have you struggled in attempting to hear God's voice?*

  ____

  ____

- *How do you feel about the prospect of God's speaking to you?*

  ____

  ____

- *Are you open to being challenged to listen more to what God may say to you?*

  ____

  ____

LESSON 2

WHY GOD SPEAKS TO US

God speaks to us for reasons that are purely His own; He loves us, and He desires to have a relationship with us. Psalm 81 is a deeply moving plea from God to His people:

Hear, O My people, and I will admonish you!
O Israel, if you will listen to Me!
There shall be no foreign god among you;
Nor shall you worship any foreign god.
I am the LORD your God,
Who brought you out of the land of Egypt;
Open your mouth wide, and I will fill it.
But My people would not heed My voice,
And Israel would have none of Me.
So I gave them over to their own stubborn heart,
To walk in their own counsels.
Oh, that My people would listen to Me,
That Israel would walk in My ways!
I would soon subdue their enemies,
And turn My hand against their adversaries.
The haters of the LORD would pretend submission to Him,
But their fate would endure forever.
He would have fed them also with the finest of wheat;

And with honey from the rock I would have satisfied you (vv. 8–16).

Can you hear the sorrow in God's voice as He pleads with His people to listen to Him? And for what purpose?

So that He might bless them! God desires only good for His people.

- *After reading Psalm 81:8–16, what new insight do you have about how God desires to relate to you?*

  ____

  ____

- *What do you believe He wants to do for you in your life right now?*

  ____

  ____

God's Desire Toward Us

God created us for fellowship, that we might be in relationship with Him. He desires to walk and talk with us, just as He did with Adam and Eve.

He loves us and desires for us to love Him in return.

He gives to us and desires that we give back to Him.

He shields us and protects us from evil and desires that we trust Him.

He provides all that we need and desires that we rely on Him as the source of our total supply.

He is our Father. We are His children. He desires that our relationship as Father and children be healthy, joyful, loving, and fulfilling.

Very specifically, God desires in His love that we might *comprehend* His truth about who He is, who we are, and the relationship He desires to have with us; be *conformed* to His truth, applying His truth to our lives in a way that transforms us ever more closely into the image of Christ Jesus; and *communicate* His truth to others.

Comprehend the Truth

God has given to all believers a divine person—the Holy Spirit—who lives within us to help us receive and understand the truth. The Holy Spirit knows perfectly the mind of God, and the Holy Spirit communicates to our spirits the truth God wants us to hear.

What the Word Says	What the Word Says to Me
The Helper, the Holy Spirit, whom the Father will send in My name, He will teach you all things, and bring to your remembrance all things that I said to you (John 14:26).	______________________
"Eye has not seen, nor ear heard, nor have entered into the heart of man the things which God has prepared for those who love Him." But God has revealed them to us through His Spirit. For the Spirit searches all things, yes, the deep things of God (1 Cor. 2:9–10).	______________________
We have received, not the spirit of the world, but the Spirit who is from God, that we might know the things that have been freely given to us by God (1 Cor. 2:12).	______________________

God desires that we know the mind of God. We can never know the mind of God fully because we are finite creatures and He is infinite. But we can grow in our understanding about who God is, how He operates in our world, and why He does the things He does.

For many reasons, we may be limited in our understanding of God's motives and methods. We may not have read all the Bible. To understand the true and full context of any passage of God's Word, we need to understand the true and full context of all God's Word. Also, we may have cultural differences that keep us from understanding fully what certain things in the Bible mean. We may not have the maturity in Christ Jesus that we need to understand deeper layers of meaning. We may be trying to understand the Bible solely with our minds, which is always futile. The Bible is a spiritual book. It speaks to and is applied to the spirit. None of these reasons, however, are a fixed wall for us. We can grow in our understanding by reading more of God's Word, studying the cultural background of the Bible, gaining more maturity in Christ Jesus, and learning how to read the Bible with spiritual understanding.

- *In your own life experience, what do you know now about the Lord and about His Word that you didn't know last year? Five years ago? Ten years ago? In what ways are you growing?*

____

____

The Truth About God

The Lord desires that we know the truth about Him.

First, He is our Creator. God fashioned us as unique creatures. He made all of the natural world for us to rule and enjoy. He has provided all that we need.

Second, He is our life. God breathed into us His breath. We are spirit because God imparted His Spirit to us. We cannot exist apart from God.

Third, He loves us. He is continually reaching out to us with affection, calling to us individually by name.

What the Word Says	What the Word Says to Me
God created man in His own image; in the image of God He created him; male and female He created them. Then God blessed them. . . Then God saw everything that He had made, and indeed it was very good (Gen. 1:27–28, 31).	
The LORD God formed man of the dust of the ground, and breathed into his nostrils the breath of life; and man became a living being (Gen. 2:7).	
We love Him because He first loved us (1 John 4:19).	

The Truth About Ourselves

The truth about ourselves is twofold.

First, the Holy Spirit convicts us that we are sinners. We are born apart from God. The primary message of the Holy Spirit to us as long as we are apart from God is that we need God.

Second, once we have accepted Jesus Christ as our Savior, the Holy Spirit becomes our Comforter and Counselor. He speaks hope to us in times of turmoil. He strengthens our faith to trust God for our total sustenance. He gives us the assurance not only of our salvation but also of God's faithfulness and total provision toward us. He reveals to us our nature as God's saints on the earth and challenges us to grow more like Jesus.

What the Word Says	What the Word Says to Me
For God so loved the world that He gave His only begotten Son,	

that whoever believes in Him should not perish but have everlasting life. For God did not send His Son into the world to condemn the world, but that the world through Him might be saved (John 3:16–17).	_______________________
Whoever confesses that Jesus is the Son of God, God abides in him, and he in God (1 John 4:15).	_______________________
Therefore, if anyone is in Christ, he is a new creation; old things have passed away; behold, all things have become new (2 Cor. 5:17).	_______________________

As we discover more about ourselves, we usually begin to see others in a new light. We see our fellow believers as people whom God is also fashioning, forming, and transforming. We see that all people are loved by God, are in need of God, and can have access to God. We become much more inclined to love others unconditionally.

I have experienced this in my life from a friend who walked through a very painful time of suffering with me. God was sifting me, sanding me, and pruning me until I thought there wouldn't be anything left of me. Sometimes I spoke harshly to my friend, but he always said to me, "I understand. What can I do to help?" He never rejected me or showed disappointment in me. No matter what I shared, he just loved me. He wept with me, prayed with me, laughed with me, and patiently listened to me. How I hope you have a friend like that in your life! How I hope you can become such a friend!

God's truth to us is that we are to love one another.

What the Word Says	What the Word Says to Me
These things I command you, that you love one another (John 15:17).	
Beloved, let us love one another, for love is of God; and everyone who loves is born of God and knows God (1 John 4:7).	
If someone says, "I love God," and hates his brother, he is a liar (1 John 4:20).	

Conformed to the Truth

It is not enough that we comprehend the truth. We must be conformed to the truth.

God calls us to present ourselves to Him as if we are a "living sacrifice." In the Old Testament days, God consumed sacrifices with His holy fire as a sign of His presence among the people. In our time, God burns out of us with His holy presence everything that is not like Jesus, and then He causes us to burn and to shine brightly with a zeal for living the life Jesus would live if He was walking in our shoes.

As we read and hear God's Word, we come face-to-face with ourselves, our deficiencies, our errors, our faults. We say again and again, "I'm not like Jesus. But I want to be like Him." At these times we know that God is truly speaking to us because God always calls us to become more and more like Jesus.

How do you do this? You say to the Father, "Help me to change. Help me to be more like Jesus." God has promised that He will show you how to be like Jesus, and He will help you become more like Him.

Every time you realize that your life doesn't line up perfectly with the truth of God's Word, you have a choice to make—to accept or reject God's way. When you accept God's way and openly say to the Lord, "I'm not like that, but I want to be like that," He begins to do something inside you. You may find that your tastes are changing. You may become uncomfortable in situations in which you used to feel comfortable. You may have new desires for things that are good, healthful, and wholesome. That's the transforming power of God at work!

What the Word Says

Do not be conformed to this world, but be transformed by the renewing of your mind, that you may prove what is that good and acceptable and perfect will of God (Rom. 12:2).

For whom He foreknew, He also predestined to be conformed to the image of His Son, that He might be the firstborn among many brethren (Rom. 8:29).

For if anyone is a hearer of the word and not a doer, he is like a man observing his natural face in a mirror; for he observes himself, goes away, and immediately forgets what kind of man he was. But he who looks into the perfect law of liberty and continues in it, and is not a forgetful hearer but a doer of the work, this one will be blessed in what he does (James 1:23–25).

What the Word Says to Me

____
____
____
____
____
____

____
____
____
____
____

____
____
____
____
____
____
____
____
____
____
____
____

Consider these questions:

- *Is there something about your life today that you know is not like Jesus? (What is the first thing that comes to mind?)*

____

____

- *Do you feel challenged to be conformed to the truth?*

____

____

Communicate the Truth

Finally, God desires that we communicate His truth to others. God does not give us His truth so that we might hoard it, but that we might share it. He does not impart blessings to us so that we might store them up, but that we might give them away to others and grow in our capacity to receive even more from God. He does not love us so that we might merely bask in His love, but that we might extend His love to others and, in so doing, draw them closer to the Lord. Jesus' commandment was this: "Go therefore and make disciples" (Matt. 28:19).

You communicate your relationship with God whether you intend to do so or not. Your actions, your demeanor, and your spontaneous words reflect your heart. But there is something beyond "simply being" that the Lord calls you to do. He desires that you actively and intentionally share what you know about God with others.

Why? So that others might come to know Him, and so that those who know Him might continue to grow in Him. But there is yet another reason—and that is so that you might have more brothers and sisters in Christ Jesus, and that your relationship with these brothers and sisters in Christ Jesus might be deeper and richer.

You see, God wants us to have a loving relationship with Him as our heavenly Father, and He desires that we have loving relationships with others so that our lives might be more joyful, meaningful, and fulfilling. We aren't called to a relationship with God in isolation. Rather, He desires that we become a family of God here on this earth—with a sense of belonging, identity, unconditional love, and great value as individuals.

When we openly and freely share the truth of God with others, we build community. We forge eternal relationships. We connect with people who also are seeking to know God's truth and be conformed to it. And in that, we find strength and comfort and mutual assistance. We become "fitted together" with others in a bond that brings us individually and collectively toward greater wholeness.

What the Word Says	What the Word Says to Me
For as the body is one and has many members, but all the members of that one body, being many, are one body, so also is Christ. . . . And if one member suffers, all the members suffer with it; or if one member is honored, all the members rejoice with it (1 Cor. 12:12, 26).	____________________
Therefore comfort each other and edify [build up, establish, improve morally] one another (1 Thess. 5:11).	____________________

You will be far less effective in communicating truth to other people if you are not personally living a life being conformed to the truth. The fact is that people see who you are far more readily than they hear what you say. To live a life of being conformed to the truth, you must first comprehena the truth. You can't become what you don't know to become. Which brings us back to the central point of this lesson. Why does God desire to speak to you? He wants to show you what He is like. He wants to reveal Himself to you.

God knows that the more you see Him for who He is, in His fullness—as your loving Father and Creator who desires only the best for you—the more you are going to want to be with Him. The more you are with Him, the more you are going to want to become like Him. The more you become like Him, the greater your witness in the world. The greater your witness, the more others will begin to hear His voice and the more enriching and loving your relationships with others will become.

God speaks to you for your benefit and for His delight in establishing a relationship with you.

Consider these questions:

- *What new insights have you gained from this lesson about God's desire to communicate with you?*

  ____

  ____

- *How do you feel today about God's desire to communicate with you?*

  ____

  ____

- *What in your background may affect that feeling?*

  ____

  ____

- *What are you challenged to do?*

  ____

  ____

LESSON 3

HOW GOD HAS SPOKEN

Through the ages, God has used a variety of ways to speak to His people. He apparently talked face-to-face on a daily basis with Adam and Eve in the Garden of Eden, meeting them in the cool of the day (Gen. 3:8). After Adam and Eve disobeyed God and were expelled from the Garden, God turned to other forms ot communication with His beloved creation.

There are at least eight ways in which God spoke to His people in Bible times:

1. Direct revelation
2. Dreams
3. Written words
4. Prophets
5. Circumstances
6. Angels
7. Jesus Christ
8. The Holy Spirit

Ways He Does Not Speak

We will explore each of these eight ways briefly in this lesson, but I would like to indicate at the outset of this study that there are two ways in which God did not and does not speak to His people.

1. God does not speak to His people through natural phenomena.

That statement may seem strange to you since many of us say that we feel closer to God when we are in the great outdoors. I am a lover of God's natural world. Few things delight me as much as seeing the beauty of nature and taking photographs of what God has created. Having feelings about God's presence and about His creation is not the same, however, as claiming that we have a message from God through some act of nature.

We cannot observe a volcanic eruption or a hurricane, for example, and say, "Look at what God is saying." Neither can we perceive a certain pattern in the ashes of a fireplace and conclude, "This is God's word." I know a man who saw a cross shape in the clouds as he was flying in a jet one day, and he concluded that it was a sign that meant he was saved. A glint in the skies does not have anything to do with confessing our sinful state, receiving God's forgiveness, or believing in Jesus Christ and confessing Him as Savior and Lord, which is the pattern that the Bible gives for our salvation.

The broad message of God in nature is that our God is an orderly God, who operates His universe according to purpose, design, and intention. We see in nature that God loves beauty and that He provides amply for His children. We see that God has seasons of timing and a rhythm of life for all things, including each of us. We see that God is infinitely creative, and certainly, as we look at some aspects of human nature, we must conclude that God has a sense of humor. Ultimately, we see in nature that God is supreme and awesome, and that we are the work of His hands, the created and not the Creator. Nature speaks of God. That is far different from saying, "God speaks through nature a personal word to us."

When we try to see God's message in natural events, we are dangerously close to the practice of divination. God clearly condemns divination—the attempt to discern God's message through such things as the pattern of tea leaves or the position of the stars.

God does not speak to us through astrology or fortune-tellers. The Bible calls these practices abominations to God.

Now, we must be very clear on this point so as not to misunderstand how God may use natural means to confirm His word to us or to reveal His timing. Jesus said that we are to be astutely aware of the "times and seasons" that lead up to the fulfillment of God's promises. We find a good example of this in 1 Kings 18. Elijah told King Ahab, "Go up, eat and drink; for there is the sound of abundance of rain." Elijah had received a message from God that the drought was ending. After Elijah said those words, he sent his servant to the top of a mountain to look toward the sea, the direction from which storms came to that area. He sent his servant seven times, and on the seventh trip, the servant reported, "There is a cloud, as small as a man's hand, rising out of the sea!" Elijah perceived that God was fulfilling His word, and he sent a message to the king, "Prepare your chariot, and go down before the rain stops you." (See 1 Kings 18:41–44.) Note that Elijah had the word of the Lord first and he was looking for the fulfillment of that word. A natural phenomenon was used to confirm what Elijah had already heard; the word of God came first. It's critical that you see this difference. Many people make a grave error in assuming that when they see some twist of a twig or a breeze from a certain direction that God is giving them a message or a sign.

2. God does not speak to His people through occult practices.

God's Word speaks strongly against conjuring spirits—such as séances—and any form of magic that might attempt to give us direction for our lives. Soothsayers and seers were among the people that God clearly told His children to avoid. We are to stay far away from such things as tarot cards, Ouija boards, crystals, magic charms, and other such paraphernalia associated with the occult. They are not methods that God has used in the past, is using today, or will ever use. They are among the methods that the enemy of your soul will use to try to deceive you into believing something that is wrong, deadly wrong.

Direct Revelation

Direct revelation may be what many people today regard as an audible voice of God. It can also be thought of as a very strong impression—one that comes unexpectedly, is absolutely clear, and is very specific.

Abraham had a direct revelation from God: "Get out of your country . . . to a land that I will show you" (Gen. 12:1).

The burning bush that Moses saw while tending sheep for his father-in-law, Jethro, is another example of direct revelation. Moses saw a bush "burning with fire, but the bush was not consumed." When God saw that Moses turned aside to look—in other words, when He knew He had Moses' attention—He called to him from the midst of the bush. He gave Moses very specific instructions about how Moses was to return to Egypt and bring the children of Israel out of Egypt. (See Ex. 3.)

Jesus apparently enjoyed direct revelation from the Father in an ongoing way because He said to His accusers one day, "I have not spoken on My own authority; but the Father who sent Me gave Me a command, what I should say and what I should speak. And I know that His command is everlasting life. Therefore, whatever I speak, just as the Father has told Me, so I speak" (John 12:49–50).

What the Word Says	**What the Word Says to Me**
Meditate on one or more of these passages:	
Genesis 12:1–2—Abraham's call	______________________
Exodus 3—the burning bush	______________________
1 Samuel 3—God calls Samuel	______________________

Dreams and Visions

God has also spoken to people through dreams and visions. We have a number of examples in the Bible.

Joseph, the eleventh son of Jacob, had two notable dreams. In one, he saw himself and his brothers binding sheaves in a field of wheat, and all of the sheaves bowed down to Joseph's sheaf. In the other dream, the sun, moon, and eleven stars bowed down to Joseph. Those were prophetic dreams about what was to happen later in Joseph's life.

Daniel had visions in which God revealed to him the destiny of the world and the empires that were to come.

Joseph, the husband of Mary, had two remarkable dreams—one in which he felt convinced that he should take Mary to be his wife, and the other in which he saw God's direction to take Mary and Jesus to Egypt.

Peter had a vision that led to his sharing the gospel with the house of Cornelius, thereby extending the gospel to all Gentiles.

Four things are important for us to recognize about dreams and visions as a source of God's word:

First, dreams and visions that bear God's direct message are very rare in a person's life. Not all dreams and visions are God's messages to us. Some dreams are of our own creation and desire. Some are the result of the mind's processing information.

Second, ask God if He wants you to reveal to others what He has shown you in a vision or dream. Not all dreams and visions are meant to be shared fully and freely with everybody in hearing range.

Third, we are never told in the Scriptures to seek dreams and visions. In no place are we commanded to pray for them or to request God to give them to us. Dreams and visions are at God's initiative.

Fourth, visions and dreams are confirmed by outward circumstances, either immediately or ultimately. If God gives a dream or vision, it comes to pass!

What the Word Says	**What the Word Says to Me**
Meditate on one or more of these passages:	
Genesis 37:5–11—Joseph's dreams	______________________ ______________________

Matthew 1:19–25; 2:13–15—dreams of Joseph, Mary's husband ______________________

Acts 10:9–34—visions of Peter and Cornelius ______________________

The Written Word of God

We read in Exodus 31:18: "And when He had made an end of speaking with him [Moses] on Mount Sinai, He gave Moses two tablets of the Testimony, tablets of stone, written with the finger of God."

God has always placed great value on the written word. In fact, the Hebrew people were among the first people on the earth to have an alphabet and to record documents. The reading of the Torah (first five books of the Old Testament) has been a mainstay in synagogue services through the centuries.

God's advice was spread throughout the early church by both spoken and written means. The gospel accounts are a written documentation of the life and words of Jesus. Much of the rest of the New Testament was originally written as letters from the apostles to the various groups of believers throughout the Roman Empire.

Behind the written Word of God is always the inspiration of God. We read in 2 Timothy 3:16: "All Scripture is given by inspiration of God, and is profitable for doctrine, for reproof, for correction, for instruction in righteousness, that the man of God may be complete, thoroughly equipped for every good work."

What the Word Says	What the Word Says to Me
Your word is a lamp to my feet And a light to my path (Ps. 119:105).	______________________

Take the helmet of salvation, and the sword of the Spirit, which is the word of God (Eph. 6:17).

The word of God is living and powerful, and sharper than any two-edged sword, piercing even to the division of soul and spirit, and of joints and marrow, and is a discerner of the thoughts and intents of the heart (Heb. 4:12).

Words of the Prophets

We repeatedly find in the Scriptures this phrase: "Thus says the Lord." Those who spoke these words of God—men and women we call prophets—seemed to have felt they had little choice in the matter. God so overwhelmingly gave them a message that they could do nothing else but speak. Isaiah spoke of it as a burning coal applied to his lips. Jeremiah said that he felt as if he had fire shut up in his bones.

Prophets did far more than foretell future events. In many ways, their words can be considered prophetic from the standpoint that they spelled out what was wrong in the people's hearts and that without repentance, certain conclusions were inevitable.

To be a prophet means ultimately to speak the truth of God to others. Sometimes, that truth is about trends or future conclusions. At other times, it is very specific truth about a particular circumstance. And at still other times, it is the telling of what God's Word says.

God continues to speak through proclaimers today—men and women we might call preachers, teachers, evangelists, Bible study leaders, Sunday school teachers, and others, people who proclaim the full story of God's truth.

We need to be very careful in discerning who is telling us the truth today. Our main source for discerning a true prophet from a false prophet is the written Word of God. We must always ask, "Is this person telling me only part of God's truth, without giving any of the consequences for not heeding God's Word?" We also must ask, "Is this person telling me something other than what I can find in the Word of God?" If so, the person isn't God's prophet.

Our second means of discernment is evidence. What a prophet says, happens. If a person tells us that God is going to do something, it must come to pass. If it doesn't, the person is a false prophet.

What the Word Says

What the Word Says to Me

Reflect upon these three "words from the Lord" by God's prophets:

Thus says the Lord GOD:
"Pound your fists and stamp your feet, and say, 'Alas, for all the evil abominations of the house of Israel! For they shall fall by the sword, by famine, and by pestilence'" (Ezek. 6:11).

The Spirit of the Lord GOD is upon Me,
Because the LORD has anointed Me
To preach good tidings to the poor;
He has sent Me to heal the brokenhearted,
To proclaim liberty to the captives,
And the opening of the prison to those who are bound;

To proclaim the acceptable year
of the LORD,
And the day of vengeance of our
God;
To comfort all who mourn,
To console those who mourn in
Zion,
To give them beauty for ashes,
The oil of joy for mourning,
The garment of praise for the
spirit of heaviness;
That they may be called trees of
righteousness,
The planting of the LORD, that
He may be glorified (Isa. 61:1–3).

Through the LORD's mercies we
are not consumed,
Because His compassions fail not.
They are new every morning;
Great is Your faithfulness.
"The LORD is my portion," says
my soul,
"Therefore I hope in Him!"
(Lam. 3:22–24).

Include in your reflection your emotional response to these prophetic words.

Circumstances That Convey Confirmation

We spoke earlier about the proper interpretation of nature. Sometimes the circumstances that God uses to confirm His word involve natural phenomena. One of the most notable examples in the Bible is the story of Gideon. Being unsure that he was hearing

God clearly and being a little fearful, Gideon asked God to confirm His word that Gideon was to lead the people in battle. He laid out a fleece one evening and asked that God make it soaking wet and the ground around it dry the following morning. Sure enough, the next morning the fleece was wet and the ground dry. Next, he asked that the fleece be dry in the midst of wet grass. Again, God graciously gave Gideon the assurance that he needed by doing as Gideon asked. (See Judg. 6:36–40.)

I never recommend that a person stipulate to God the way, means, or method that God should use to confirm His word. We are not in a position to require God to do our bidding before we obey Him. Our position is to trust Him and take Him at His word, obey, and then leave the consequences up to Him.

I believe we can, however, ask God to confirm His word to us. But we must leave the methodology up to Him!

We can regard many of the miracles in the Bible as God's use of circumstances to confirm the good news of the gospel message. They convey the message, "Yea, and amen." They underscore the direct mandates of God, provide a second witness that God has spoken, or give evidence that the gospel has been preached fully.

What the Word Says	What the Word Says to Me
They stayed there a long time, speaking boldly in the Lord, who was bearing witness to the word of His grace, granting signs and wonders to be done by their hands (Acts 14:3).	______________________
How shall we escape if we neglect so great a salvation, which at the first began to be spoken by the Lord, and was confirmed to us by those who heard Him, God	______________________

also bearing witness both with signs and wonders, with various miracles, and gifts of the Holy Spirit, according to His own will? (Heb. 2:3–4).

I have reason to glory in Christ Jesus in the things which pertain to God. For I will not dare to speak of any of those things which Christ has not accomplished through me, in word and deed, to make the Gentiles obedient— in mighty signs and wonders, by the power of the Spirit of God, so that . . . I have fully preached the gospel of Christ (Rom. 15:17–19).

Consider this question:

- *In your personal experience, how has God confirmed His word to you?*

Angelic Messages

The word *angel* means "messenger from God." God spoke through an angel to the parents of Samson, to Mary, to Peter, and to a number of other people in the Bible.

God sends angels at His will and for His purposes. We are not to seek or pray for angelic encounters. Many people today have been duped into thinking that they can call angels or conjure them up. They may be conjuring spirits all right, but let me assure you, the visages that appear to them are not God's angels. God's angels come to people uninvited, unannounced, and unexpectedly. They usually are so awesome in form that their first words are, "Fear not." They deliver their messages—which are always very direct and specific—and then leave. They do not engage in small talk, develop a friendship with a human being, or give ongoing guidance and help.

Angels appear to men and women throughout Scripture, but if you closely analyze their appearances, they appear in nearly all instances to people who are isolated from fellowship with a larger body of God-fearing people or who have no other means of hearing God's message.

The Bible refers to angels as "ministering spirits"—in other words, God sends them to help us. But they always come to us at God's choosing and on the authority of heaven. They do not appear when we think we need help; rather, they appear when God thinks we need their special help.

Our response to angels must always be, "I will do what God says." We are not to worship angels. We are to worship God alone, and we are to give all our praise to Him.

Furthermore, angels are not dead human beings. Angels are of a different creative order. People do not become angels when they die and go to heaven. People are saints, and the Scriptures tell us that saints will one day rule over angels, although we presently have less power and wisdom than the angels have. Angels are strictly the servants of God. We are sons and daughters of the almighty heavenly Father.

Finally, many people of faith in the Bible did not receive messages from angels. A visit from an angel is not a badge of approval from God.

What the Word Says	**What the Word Says to Me**
Meditate on one or more of these passages:	
Judges 13—Samson's mother	____________________

Luke 1:26–38—Gabriel to Mary	______________________
Acts 12:1–11—Peter in prison	______________________
Note especially the responses	______________________
made by these people.	______________________

Jesus Christ Is God's Word Made Flesh

God has spoken to us through His Son, Jesus Christ. He is God's supreme Word to us, a Word that appeared in fleshly form. He embodies everything that God desires to say to humankind—everything we need to know about God's nature, our nature, and the relationship He desires us to have with Him and with each other. He is God's full expression of love, care, tenderness, provision for salvation, righteousness, holiness, presence, power, and relationship. As Jesus said of Himself, He is "the way, the truth, and the life" (John 14:6).

If you have any doubt about what God wants you to do in a particular situation, look to the life of Jesus. Do what He did. If you have any doubt about how to respond to a situation or circumstance, look to Jesus. Imitate Him.

The only way in which you are not to be like Jesus is that you do not have the responsibility for dying as a sacrifice for the sins of the world. Jesus did that once—definitively. You are not anybody's savior or deliverer. Jesus alone paid that price. However, you are to take up your cross daily and follow the Lord, pouring out the very essence of your life to bring others to Him.

God has spoken through the life of Jesus Christ the perfect fulfillment of all His laws and commandments. Jesus is the Word of God made flesh.

What the Word Says	What the Word Says to Me
The Word became flesh and	______________________
dwelt among us, and we beheld	______________________

His glory, the glory as of the only begotten of the Father, full of grace and truth (John 1:14).

Jesus said to him [Thomas], "I am the way, the truth, and the life. No one comes to the Father except through Me. If you had known Me, you would have known My Father also; and from now on you know Him and have seen Him" (John 14:6–7).

The Holy Spirit Conveys God's Truth

We will discuss more about the work of the Holy Spirit in speaking God's word to us in the next lesson, but let it suffice for now that we recognize that God speaks to each believer by His Holy Spirit. What assurance that should give to us! We have direct and immediate access to God's opinion at all times. We have the full counsel of God available to us. We have His presence abiding within us to lead, guide, comfort, encourage, correct, and challenge us. The Holy Spirit is, indeed, "God with us."

What the Word Says | **What the Word Says to Me**

I will pray the Father, and He will give you another Helper, that He may abide with you forever—the Spirit of truth, whom the world cannot receive, because it neither sees Him nor knows Him; but you know Him, for He dwells with you and will be in you. I will not leave you orphans;

I will come to you (John 14:16–18).

Jesus said to them again, "Peace to you! As the Father has sent Me, I also send you." And when He had said this, He breathed on them, and said to them, "Receive the Holy Spirit" (John 20:21–22).

You shall receive power when the Holy Spirit has come upon you; and you shall be witnesses to Me in Jerusalem, and in all Judea and Samaria, and to the end of the earth (Acts 1:8).

Consider these questions:

- *What insights have you gained about the ways in which God has spoken to people through the ages?*

- *With which of God's methods of communication would you feel most comfortable? Why?*

LESSON 4

THE PRIMARY WAYS GOD SPEAKS TODAY

In the last lesson, we explored eight ways in which God has spoken to men and women through the ages. We must never limit God in the methods that He uses to speak to us, but from my experience and observation, I believe there are three main ways that God speaks to us today:

1. His Word
2. His Holy Spirit
3. Other believers in Christ Jesus

The person who desires to hear from God, and who wants to put himself or herself into the best position to hear from God, will follow one of these three methods. In these ways God routinely, daily, and consistently speaks to all people who seek Him.

Listening to God Through the Bible

It is no accident that the Bible is so routinely called the Word of God. The Bible is God's foremost way today of communicating with us.

In the Bible, we have the complete revelation of God. He doesn't need to add anything else to this book. Through the ages, the revelation of God was an unfolding truth by God about Himself. In Jesus, that truth was fulfilled. As Jesus said of Himself, He didn't come to change anything about the law or the commandments; He came to show us by His life's example how to fully live out God's plan in our lives. (See Matt. 5:17.)

God's Word is for all people because it speaks to the basic human condition. The Bible addresses every emotion, human relationship dynamic, problem of the heart, aspect of the psyche, temptation or desire, heartache or joy, or issue of faith, love, or hope.

In the Old Testament, we have God's laws and commands, complete with examples of how God works in relationship to His own law and what happens when humankind disobeys the law (or obeys it). We have songs and poetry that tell us about the nature of God and the nature of people, and the nature of the relationship God desires with humankind. We have promises of God's presence.

In the New Testament, we see how God gave us His Son, Jesus Christ, to live out God's plan before us—becoming our role model, mentor, older brother and, ultimately, our Savior and the door through which we enter eternal life. We see what happened to the first disciples and apostles as they received the promised Holy Spirit and began to live the very life of Christ Jesus in their society. We find teachings that show us how the Holy Spirit enables us to live a life that is fully pleasing to God the Father, a life that goes beyond mere law because it is based on the spirit of God's law, not the letter of the law.

The Bible covers it all! What a precious gift to us! Whenever we face difficulties, experience heartaches, or have questions, we should go first to the Scriptures. There God will speak to us directly, personally, intimately, and effectively.

How does this work in a practical way? First, you pray and seek God's guidance about a decision. You should ask boldly for God to speak to you through His Word and give you His wisdom. (See James 1:5–6.)

In response to your prayer, the Lord often will direct your mind to a particular passage of Scripture that you have encountered in your regular daily reading of the Bible. He will bring to your remembrance His truth on the matter.

If you do not hear from God about precisely where to turn in the Scriptures, you should begin to read the words of Jesus. (I suggest you read a Bible that has the words of Jesus printed in red ink; that makes it very easy to see what Jesus had to say.) As you read, you may become intrigued with a particular line of thought, or you may be drawn to a particular word or phrase. You may want to use a concordance at that point to discover other places in God's Word where that word or phrase is used. Follow the lead that you sense.

In many cases, I have found that we may not go directly to the passage that holds God's truth for us in a given circumstance; rather, as we continue to read and study, God leads us step-by-step to the information He wants us to see with new spiritual insight.

Eventually, you will come to an incident in Scripture, a passage, or even a single verse that is directly related to your concern, question, or problem. It may deal with your specific experience in a way that seems uncanny or very familiar to you. Or the passage may deal in principle. You may find the key concepts that speak to your need.

As you pray and read, trust the Holy Spirit to quicken your spirit to His truth. You may feel this as a warmth inside, or you may feel a great sense of absoluteness about a particular verse. Sometimes the words on the page of your Bible may seem to stand out to you as if they were written in bold headlines. Sometimes you may not be able to get away from a particular passage. It comes repeatedly to your mind, and you can't seem to shake it from memory.

Do not limit your search of God's Word, of course, to times of crisis or need. Read His Word daily. It is as you read daily that God directs you, challenges you, warns you, comforts you, and assures you. Daily reading is like preventive spiritual health care. How much better it is to divert a problem or to address a matter before it truly becomes an issue. In your daily reading, God refines you bit by bit, slowly and yet always transforming your thoughts and responses into those of Jesus. As you read the Word daily, you store God's Word in your memory, almost as if you are making daily deposits in a bank, so that the Holy Spirit can bring to your remembrance God's Word immediately and precisely.

Don't fail to read God's Word daily. Go to it as if it is eternal nourishment for your eternal soul.

When you face a difficult situation or a problem for which you have no answer, go to God's Word first. Seek out His counsel. Jesus said, "Seek, and you will find" (Matt. 7:7).

- *In your faith walk, have you experienced times when the Word of God seemed to speak to you personally—perhaps a verse in the Bible seemed to have been written with only you in mind?*

  ____

  ____

- *How did you feel when God spoke to you in this way?*

  ____

  ____

What the Word Says	**What the Word Says to Me**
Be strong and very courageous, that you may observe to do according to all the law which Moses My servant commanded you; do not turn from it to the right hand or to the left, that you may prosper wherever you go. This Book of the Law shall not depart from your mouth, but you shall meditate in it day and night, that you may observe to do according to all that is written	_ _

in it. For then you will make your way prosperous, and then you will have good success (Josh. 1:7–8).

If any of you lacks wisdom, let him ask of God, who gives to all liberally and without reproach, and it will be given to him. But let him ask in faith, with no doubting (James 1:5–6).

Listening to the Holy Spirit

As we walk in the Spirit daily, surrendered to His power, we have the right and privilege to expect anything we need to hear from God. The Holy Spirit living within us and speaking to us ought to be the natural lifestyle of believers. We claim His presence, direction, and guidance by faith.

One of the lines of the Lord's Prayer points toward our daily reliance on the Holy Spirit: "Do not lead us into temptation, but deliver us from the evil one." I believe that is how the Holy Spirit guides us in an ongoing way each day. He speaks in our hearts a no to everything that would bring us harm, and thus, He delivers us from evil and away from temptation. He also speaks in our hearts a yes to everything that will bring us blessing.

In the Old Testament when men such as King David inquired of the Lord, the question was nearly always put to the Lord in such a way that the answer was yes or no. I believe this is the foremost way that the Holy Spirit speaks to us hour by hour as we walk through our particular set of circumstances. We can never ask too many times of the Holy Spirit, "Should I do this—yes or no?" or "Should I say this—yes or no?" We will sense in our spirits His word of reply to us. Generally, it will be a sense of enthusiasm and eager desire marked with great joy and freedom, or it will be a sense of foreboding, danger, caution, or need for silence. I find that it is much easier to receive the direction of the Holy Spirit by asking for yes-or-no counsel than to say to Him in general terms, "What do You want me to do?"

Very specifically, the Bible teaches us that the Holy Spirit guides us and gives us God's advice in these ways:

The Holy Spirit reminds us of what God has said to us and done for us in the past (including God's word to us in the Scriptures and through the life of Jesus). Jesus said that the Holy Spirit would testify of Him—in other words, remind His disciples of all that Jesus said and did, and of its appropriateness for their lives. (See John 15:26–27.) Ask the Holy Spirit to remind you continually about what Jesus would be, say, and do if He was walking in your shoes, through your circumstances, today.

The Holy Spirit gives us words to say. After describing for His disciples what would happen at the "end of the age," Jesus encouraged His disciples that the Holy Spirit would teach them what to say in moments of crisis or questioning. We, too, should breathe a prayer for the Holy Spirit to give us the words when we face difficult moments in which we don't know what to say. We can trust God to provide words for us just as surely as we can trust God to meet our other needs. At times, the Holy Spirit may advise us to remain silent.

The Holy Spirit gives us direction about where to go. The apostle Paul said that the Holy Spirit spoke to him when he was on his way to Asia, forbidding him to go there. (See Acts 16:6–7.) We can trust the Holy Spirit to point us in the right direction.

The Holy Spirit guides our prayer. Paul taught the Romans, "He [the Spirit] makes intercession for the saints according to the will of God" (Rom. 8:27). When we don't know how to pray, we should ask the Holy Spirit to pray for us and through us to the Father. That's the sure way we can know that we are always praying in God's will.

As you pray about a particular matter, ask the Holy Spirit to guide your prayer. Wait in silence for Him to bring to your mind and heart various aspects of a situation or of a person's need. You may be surprised at the things the Holy Spirit prompts you to pray—things you had never thought about before.

What the Word Says	What the Word Says to Me
When they bring you to the synagogues and magistrates and authorities, do not worry about how or what you should answer, or what you should say. For the Holy Spirit will teach you in that very hour what you ought to say (Luke 12:11–12).	
Now when they had gone through Phrygia and the region of Galatia, they were forbidden by the Holy Spirit to preach the word in Asia (Acts 16:6).	
The Spirit also helps in our weaknesses. For we do not know what we should pray for as we ought, but the Spirit Himself makes intercession for us with groanings which cannot be uttered (Rom. 8:26).	

Listening to the Word Through Other Believers

God uses people to speak to you. Some may be total strangers. Others may be dear friends or members of your immediate family. He uses pastors and teachers and Bible study group leaders.

I have been privileged to receive the wise counsel of many people of faith whom I admire and respect. Several years ago, I felt impressed to call together several men to whom I opened my heart fully and shared the deepest wounds and hurts of my life. The men heard me with love and compassion. I then said to them, "Whatever you tell me to do, I will do." They gave me counsel that was truly God's wisdom, and as they prayed for me, God broke into some of the secret areas of my heart and healed me in ways I hadn't even known were possible. I experienced God's love for me in a personal way, and with such great warmth and approval, that I have never been the same since. God used those men to speak truth to me and to be God's voice to me.

God not only gives you comfort and counsel through the words of other believers, but at times, He uses people to give you words of admonition. You need to be open to these words, also. Sometimes others can see far more clearly the mistakes you are about to make or have made.

As you open yourself up to hear God's word from other people, you must make certain that

- the word given to you is in total alignment with God's written Word, the Bible. God doesn't forget what He has already said. He doesn't contradict Himself. If a word is from God, it will be consistent with what God has already revealed through Scripture and the life of His Son, the Lord Jesus Christ.
- the person has no ulterior personal motive. When you are confused, in pain, or in need, you are much more subject to manipulation than you might be at other times. Make certain that the person who gives you counsel or advice doesn't want something from you and isn't trying to manipulate you for his or her purposes. Make certain, also, that the person turns all praise and thanksgiving toward the Lord Jesus and not toward himself or herself.
- the word does not include something that might harm another person. God doesn't cause one of His children to be blessed or to prosper at the expense of another. He doesn't move a person into a situation or circumstance that will cause another person pain, loss, or

suffering. If someone advises you to take action that will damage or destroy another person—reputation, property, relationships, spiritual growth—don't take that advice. It is not godly counsel.

- the word is for your ultimate and eternal good. God does not deal in short-term gains with long-term disasters. He always speaks to you in a way that prepares you for eternity with Him. If someone gives you advice that seems to bring a great immediate blessing, but that carries the risk of long-range detriment, refuse the advice. God's word is always consistent over time.

We must recognize that virtually all of us first came to believe in Christ Jesus because somebody told us about Jesus. Few people have a direct revelation of Christ Jesus or encounter Him first and solely in the Bible. Most of us hear the Bible preached in a way that woos us to Jesus as the Christ. Or we hear a person's testimony. The highest and best thing any of us can do is tell others about what Jesus Christ did for them on the cross.

What the Word Says

One of the two who heard John speak, and followed Him, was Andrew, Simon Peter's brother. He first found his own brother Simon, and said to him, "We have found the Messiah" (which is translated, the Christ). And he brought him to Jesus (John 1:40–42).

Now Peter and John went up together to the temple at the hour

What the Word Says to Me

of prayer, the ninth hour. And a certain man lame from his mother's womb was carried, whom they laid daily at the gate of the temple which is called Beautiful, to ask alms from those who entered the temple; who, seeing Peter and John about to go into the temple, asked for alms. And fixing his eyes on him, with John, Peter said, "Look at us." So he gave them his attention, expecting to receive something from them. Then Peter said, "Silver and gold I do not have, but what I do have I give you: In the name of Jesus Christ of Nazareth, rise up and walk." And he took him by the right hand and lifted him up, and immediately his feet and ankle bones received strength. So he, leaping up, stood and walked and entered the temple with them—walking, leaping, and praising God (Acts 3:1–8).

We know that all things work together for good to those who love God, to those who are the called according to His purpose (Rom. 8:28).

Listening to Two or More Witnesses

Look for God to confirm His Word. He may direct you to two or more passages of the Bible that convey the same meaning. He may cause you to hear a sermon or a Bible lesson that is right in line with what He has said to you in His Word. He may bring a total stranger across your path to speak a word that seems amazingly on target with last Sunday's sermon. He may use a friend to speak to you or direct you to a verse of Scripture. These multiple messages to you are part of God's assurance plan that He is the One who is speaking and that He desires for you to get the message without question or equivocation.

Consider these questions:

- *What new insights have you gained about the way God desires to speak to you today?*

____

____

- *What has God said to you recently? What method did He use?*

____

____

- *How do you feel when someone comes to you with a word of encouragement from the Lord? Counsel? Admonition or warning?*

____

____

- *In what areas do you feel challenged to explore further what God may desire to say to you?*

____

____

LESSON 5

How God Gets Our Attention

When we walk in the Spirit, our spiritual antennae alert to God, we hear what He is saying to us as a natural part of our spiritual walk. This is the Christian life, living keenly responsive to the voice of God in whatever fashion He may choose to speak to us. We can have our attention focused on a person, a chore, or an idea, but at the same time, we are so tuned to God's voice that if He speaks to us, we immediately turn our attention to Him.

Unfortunately, there are times when we choose to do things our own way. As a result, we are headed in a direction that will bring us to disaster or disappointment. God is speaking, but we aren't listening. We aren't tuned in to Him.

In these times, God often uses unusual means to get our attention. Prominent among them, from my experience and understanding of God's Word, are these four means:

1. A restless spirit
2. An unsolicited word from another person
3. Unusual circumstances—both bad and good
4. Unanswered prayers

When we look back at our lives, we nearly always can find examples of times in which God got our attention through one of these methods. His prodding may have been profound or gentle. Regardless of the intensity of His wake-up call, we awoke! And once awake, we were more than willing to hear.

As we begin this lesson, we need to be aware that although God uses these methods to get our attention, they don't necessarily have a meaning in and of themselves. In other words, we should not conclude that because we have a restless spirit, we are on the right track or the wrong track. I have met people who have concluded that if they have a certain amount of nervous energy about something, it must be right. I have also met people who automatically have decided that if they feel agitated in spirit, they are sinning. A restless spirit is an attention-getter. The message that follows is what is important! Certainly, the conscience may prick us about a matter so that we feel upset in our spirits, but the upset is not the message. The conscience is based upon our understanding of right and wrong, and that understanding is rightly based upon the truth found in the Bible.

Sometimes the Lord will prompt a person to say something to us that is *exactly* what we need to hear. The other person may not realize he is being used by God in this way, or he may be speaking to a group and have no idea he is speaking directly to us. The message, however, hits us right between the eyes. It gets our attention.

Unusual circumstances must be treated like a restless spirit. Great blessings are not an automatic message that God is pleased with you. The message that follows from such an outpouring in your life may not be that God is pleased; it may be that God wants you to do something very specific with the blessings. A tragedy is not God's curse on your life. Rather, you should perceive it as your opportunity to come before God to hear what He has to say to you in the midst of your need.

In the matter of prayer, sometimes we are so eager to hear the answer we want to hear that we fail to hear God's answer. We perceive in these cases that our prayer has gone unanswered. Although our perception is not accurate, it can lead us to question further, "Why am I not hearing from You, God?" Such questioning, done in an honest and soul-searching manner, can lead us to the position where we do hear God's voice.

Restlessness of Spirit

The sixth chapter of Esther has an excellent example of God using a restless spirit to get a person's attention. King Ahasuerus had been unwittingly duped by his prime minister, Haman. Haman hated all Jews, especially Queen Esther's relative, Mordecai. He tricked the king into signing an edict for the annihilation of the Jews. After he signed the proclamation, the king could not sleep. He had a restless spirit to the point that he "commanded to bring the book of the records of the chronicles; and they were read before the king" (Est. 6:1). The king discovered during that sleepless night that Mordecai had saved the king's life earlier by reporting an assassination plot. Instead of the Jews being killed, Mordecai was honored and Haman faced the gallows.

In my life, God frequently uses a persistent restlessness to direct me. When I look back over my life and ministry, I can see clearly that every time God moved me from one pastorate to another, He caused me to feel restless for several months beforehand. That restlessness drove me to seek God so that when the time came, I was ready to hear Him.

A restlessness of spirit is not a case of nerves. It's much deeper than that. This type of restlessness originates in the deepest aspect of a person's being as part anticipation, part uneasiness. It persists over time.

When you have that feeling, the best thing for you to do is to stop and ask the Lord what He is trying to say. Spend even more time in the Word and in prayer. Don't attempt to outrun this feeling or to throw yourself into some activity just to keep busy and to keep your mind occupied. Do just the opposite. Consider a time of fasting (food, activities, time, or a combination of these). Set aside a block of time—perhaps a weekend, several days, or even a week or two—to quiet yourself before the Lord so you can hear from Him clearly.

- *Have you ever experienced a restless spirit? What did you do about it? What was the outcome?*

____

____

What the Word Says	What the Word Says to Me
Why do You stand afar off, O LORD? Why do You hide in times of trouble? . . . Arise, O LORD! O God, lift up Your hand! Do not forget the humble. . . . The LORD is King forever and ever (Ps. 10:1, 12, 16).	
Read this entire psalm. What range and progression of emotions does the psalmist seem to feel? Can you sense his restlessness?	

A Word from Others

I don't know anybody who enjoys hearing a word of admonition. We may *say* that we appreciate words of correction or warning, but we usually feel uncomfortable when they come. We don't like to hear about sin or its consequences, especially if the person is talking about our sin.

King David was in such a position when the prophet Nathan confronted him about his sin with Bathsheba and his subsequent sin against Uriah. David apparently continued his reign without any visible evidence of a guilty conscience. And then in 2 Samuel 12:1 we read, "Then the LORD sent Nathan to

David. And he came to him, and said to him..." David desperately needed to hear what Nathan said to him, but it wasn't a pleasant experience for him.

Not all messages from others are negative, however. I can remember a person saying something to me that was very positive. I wasn't at all expecting a compliment or word of affirmation, although I desperately needed one at the time. The statement was not in response to anything that I had done or said to the person. The person's positive word, so specific and so direct, caught me off guard. When I questioned God about it, He let me see that He cared so much about me that He used a person who was almost a stranger to tell me so, in order that He might startle me into paying attention!

Sometimes we lightly dismiss compliments and words of appreciation or approval. The words of blessing may also be God's way of getting our attention off our pity party to see our true worth in His eyes. The person who cannot receive heartfelt thanks or affirming words is often the person who most needs such positive edification.

At the opposite end of the spectrum, the person who cannot take criticism or reproof is destined for failure. That message is repeated often in the book of Proverbs.

In either case—whether with words of reproof or praise—you must be extremely careful that others do not lead you astray with their words. People can use flattery, veiled threats, or even Scriptures to get you to fulfill their desires or do their bidding, all in the name of God. When someone comes to you with a message from God, take a close look at both the message and the messenger. Carefully weigh what the person says. And then go to God's Word and ask the Lord to speak to you directly. Count the praise or admonition of others only as an attention-getter that causes you to seek God.

Sometimes the message that comes to you is one of information. You may be puzzled, concerned, frustrated, or worried by what you hear. At these times, turn to God. See what He desires to say to you about the situation, about whether you are to act, and if so, in what way and when. That's what Nehemiah did when Hanani, one of his brethren, came from Judah with a report about the distress of the people in Jerusalem and about the broken-down state of Jerusalem's walls and gates. (See Neh. 1:1–11.)

The word you receive from someone may represent a need in God's kingdom, the plight of fellow believers, or a specific plea for help in extending the gospel. If your heart is touched by the matter, or if you can't seem to shake the message that you have heard, take the matter before the Lord to hear what He has to say to you about ways in which you should become involved.

- *Has someone ever come to you with a "word from the Lord" about your life?*

- *How did you feel when that happened?*

- *What did you do? What was the outcome?*

What the Word Says

So it was, when I heard these words, that I sat down and wept, and mourned for many days; I was fasting and praying before the God of heaven (Neh. 1:4).

Read 2 Chronicles 10. Note the short-term and long-term consequences of Rehoboam's failure to heed the elders of Israel.

What the Word Says to Me

Read 2 Kings 17:7–16. How would you have felt if a prophet had arrived on your doorstep with this message?

____
____
____
____

Circumstances

Circumstances can set us up to open our hearts to God and turn our attention fully toward Him.

I have seen numerous examples in my ministry of illness, accidents, bankruptcies, failures, divorces, disappointments, and other times of trouble bringing people to their knees and to a total reliance on Christ—sometimes for the first time in their lives, sometimes for a renewal of surrender and commitment. These situations are not necessarily caused by God. They may not be the result of our own error or sin. But they are circumstances in which we question life and seek answers, and very often, that search for meaning turns us toward our heavenly Father and gives Him a greater opportunity to speak to us.

When trouble strikes, your first response should never be, "Why, God?" or "Why me, God?" There is no good answer to such questions in most cases. Your first response should be, "What do You have to say to me in the midst of this, God?" He *will* speak.

Unusual circumstances can also be in the form of blessings. This is certainly the type of attention-getting method I enjoy most! The apostle Paul described this form of attention-getting in Romans 2:4: "Do you despise the riches of His goodness, forbearance, and longsuffering, not knowing that the goodness of God leads you to repentance?" The blessings may be spiritual or financial, or they may involve your home or vocation. God just seems to pile on the blessings. If you are not careful, you may assume that you have a right to use these blessings in any way you desire. Instead, you need to ask the Lord *why* He is blessing you so abundantly. He may very well have a special plan for you to use these blessings for the furtherance of His kingdom, and if you fail to be sensitive to God's plan, you can miss an even greater blessing ahead.

- *Has an unusual set of circumstances ever led you to seek God in a new way? What happened when you opened your ears to hear God's voice?*

____

____

What the Word Says

Then He said, "Go out, and stand on the mountain before the LORD." And behold, the LORD passed by, and a great and strong wind tore into the mountains and broke the rocks in pieces before the LORD, but the LORD was not in the wind; and after the wind an earthquake, but the LORD was not in the earthquake; and after the earthquake a fire, but the LORD was not in the fire; and after the fire a still small voice. So it was, when Elijah heard it, that he wrapped his face in his mantle and went out and stood in the entrance of the cave (1 Kings 19:11–13).

What the Word Says to Me

Unanswered Prayer

When all of our prayers seem to be answered, we may become complacent and just cruise through life without paying close attention to what God desires to say to us. Then we encounter a particularly urgent need, and the heavens seem to be made of brass. The silence is uncomfortable to us. We feel a growing desperation to hear from God. At that time, God has our full attention, to be sure!

There are legitimate reasons in the Scriptures why some requests are not granted:

- A person may be asking for the wrong reasons (James 4:3).
- A person may be in disobedience or rebellion (1 John 3:22).
- A person may be asking for something that is outside the will of God (1 John 5:14).
- A person may be in a state of unforgiveness with another person (Matt. 6:14–15).

Peter taught that husbands are to dwell with their wives "with understanding, giving honor to the wife, as to the weaker vessel, and as being heirs together of the grace of life, that your prayers may not be hindered" (1 Peter 3:7).

At times, God refuses to answer our prayers because He knows that if He answers them, we will stray farther off base. For example, an answered prayer may cause us to respond with personal pride and error in thinking that our prayers alone led to a miracle, a healing, a blessing, or a person's salvation.

We need to keep in mind, of course, that what we call an unanswered prayer may be a "no," a "not now," or a "not until" answer. Each is a valid answer, although it may not be the answer we desire. The Lord denied Paul's request for the removal of his "thorn" of the flesh, and He gave instead a "grace sufficient" to help Paul face and overcome his problem. (See 2 Cor. 12:7–9.) Not all prayer is answered with a yes. Sometimes no is the best answer for our situation.

- *Have you ever experienced a time when heaven seemed to be silent? In hindsight, was there a reason?*

____

____

- *Was the answer perhaps no? How did you feel when this happened?*

____

____

- *What did you do? What was the outcome?*

____

____

What the Word Says	What the Word Says to Me
I cry out to You, but You do not answer me; I stand up, and You regard me (Job 30:20).	______________________ ______________________ ______________________
Read 2 Corinthians 12:2–10. What role does suffering play in our lives?	______________________ ______________________ ______________________

No Such Thing as an Accident

There is no such thing as an accident with God. He has a plan and purpose for our lives, and even when bad things happen to us or around us, we can trust that God is continuing to work for our benefit. Our role is not to flail our arms against a tragedy but to lift our arms to God so that He might reach down and lift us up, hold us close, and speak His words to us.

God may use one method to get your attention in one circumstance and a different method at another time. Or He may consistently use one method to get your attention to the point that whenever you feel restless, or you face unusual circumstances, you automatically say, "I wonder what God wants to say to me?" Don't try to second-guess God, however. Recognize that He is a creative God and that He uses many methods to reach us and guide us.

Recognize, too, that God doesn't use the same methods for all people in like circumstances. He knows exactly how to reach each person. We err in prayer when we attempt to dictate to God how He should get the attention of another person.

God cares enough to employ various and sundry methods to cause us to stop and listen to what He is saying. He does not let us walk into an open manhole, spiritually speaking, without giving us clearly discernible danger signs. He never quits trying to reach us so that He can guide us into His wonderful plans and purposes for our lives.

Consider these questions:

- *What new insights have you gained about how God gets our attention?*

  ____

  ____

- *In your experience, is there one way in which God consistently seems to get your attention?*

  ____

  ____

- *How do you feel when you realize that you have not been listening as closely as you might have listened? How do you feel when you realize that God has not given up in trying to reach you with His plans for your good?*

  ____

  ____

- *Do you feel challenged that God may be trying to get your attention right now?*

  ____

  ____

LESSON 6

THE HALLMARKS OF GOD'S MESSAGES TO US

Jesus said of those who follow Him,

> My sheep hear My voice, and I know them, and they follow Me. And I give them eternal life, and they shall never perish; neither shall anyone snatch them out of My hand. My Father, who has given them to Me, is greater than all; and no one is able to snatch them out of My Father's hand (John 10:27–29).

What a great statement of hope and comfort that is to us! We can know the voice of the Lord. As we follow His voice and do what He says to do, we will never perish, and neither will we ever be snatched out of His hand.

"But," you may say, "how can I be sure that the voice I'm hearing is truly the voice of God?"

There are five identifying hallmarks of God's messages to us. They are a means of determining whether the voice that we are hearing is truly the voice of God. If you have questions about whether a message is from God, line it up against these criteria:

1. The message must be consistent with the Word of God, the Bible.
2. The message will usually be in conflict with the mainstream of conventional human wisdom.
3. The message will clash with fleshly gratification and basic human lusts.
4. The message will challenge one's faith to rise to a new level.
5. The message will call for personal courage to do what God has said to do, or to change in one's life what God has said to change.

As we begin our study of these identifying traits of God's messages, let me point out that the first of them, consistency with the written Word, is always our first recourse in determining the validity of a message we believe to be from God. God never contradicts Himself. What He has set forth as truth in the past is truth now.

A passage for you to keep in mind as we take a look at these identifying traits is this:

> *"For My thoughts are not your thoughts,*
> *Nor are your ways My ways," says the LORD.*
> *"For as the heavens are higher than the earth,*
> *So are My ways higher than your ways,*
> *And My thoughts than your thoughts" (Isa. 55:8–9).*

God operates at a supremely higher plane than we do. His motives toward us are always pure and loving; His ideals are the most noble of all; His holiness is absolute. What God says to us is never going to be what we perceive to be customary or the norm of our humanity. God doesn't stoop to our level. He calls us to rise to His level. His messages challenge us to live up to the high calling of a life in Christ Jesus, to pursue wholeness, and to seek the fullness of our potential in Him.

Keep in mind, also, that God doesn't call us to become something that He doesn't enable us to become. He doesn't ask us to do things that He won't equip us to do. He doesn't hold out a goal for us that is impossible for us to reach. God's messages to us will challenge us to be the best that we can be in Him and to open our lives to receive the best that He has for us.

What the Word Says	What the Word Says to Me
Therefore you shall be perfect, just as your Father in heaven is perfect (Matt. 5:48).	______________________
One thing I do, forgetting those things which are behind and reaching forward to those things which are ahead, I press toward the goal for the prize of the upward call of God in Christ Jesus (Phil. 3:13–14).	______________________
He made Him who knew no sin to be sin for us, that we might become the righteousness of God in Him (2 Cor. 5:21).	______________________

Consistency with the Bible

God will never tell us to engage in any activity or enter into any relationship that is inconsistent with holy Scripture. That is why if we neglect the Word of God and don't build it into our lives on a daily basis, we can easily be deceived. We won't be able to tell if a message is out of line with God's Word unless we know God's Word.

If you are in the process of making a decision about a relationship, a business matter, a new direction in your life, or any major change, start your decision-making process in God's Word. Go to the Word of God and stay there until you see clearly what God says about the matter.

You may have noted that when you are challenged in this study to take a look at Scripture and respond to it, you are usually given more than one verse to read. When you take the meaning of one verse and add it to the meaning of another verse and add it to the meaning of yet other verses, you build a foundation of meaning. You understand far more clearly the full wisdom of God on a particular matter.

You err when you come to God's Word with preconceived answers and predisposed attitudes, and say, "I'm looking for proof that what I believe is right." You are in a far stronger position before the Lord when you come to His Word asking humbly and honestly, "Teach me Your ways, God. Show me what You want me to see," and then let the Word speak to you in its fullness.

What the Word Says	**What the Word Says to Me**
Good and upright is the LORD; Therefore He teaches sinners in the way. The humble He guides in justice, And the humble He teaches His way. All the paths of the LORD are mercy and truth, To such as keep His covenant and His testimonies (Ps. 25:8–10).	______________________
Be diligent to present yourself approved to God, a worker who does not need to be ashamed, rightly dividing the word of truth. But shun profane and idle	______________________

babblings, for they will increase to more ungodliness. And their message will spread like cancer (2 Tim. 2:15–17).

The word of the LORD was to them,
"Precept upon precept, precept upon precept,
Line upon line, line upon line,
Here a little, there a little" (Isa. 28:13).

Conflict with Worldly, Conventional Wisdom

God's wisdom is not the same as the world's conventional wisdom. If a person has grown up in a godly home, attended church all his life, and lived in a community that had a high percentage of God-fearing, Christ-following people, he may have a different understanding of human wisdom from that of a person who grew up in an ungodly atmosphere, never attended church, and lived in a sinful environment. The godly person who is surrounded with godly people may become a little naive about what the world is like, and he may say, "Well, what I hear God saying to me is what I've heard all my life." That person needs to recognize that he has been blessed or that his situation is relatively rare.

In most cases, God's message stands in sharp contrast to what the world around us has to say on an issue.

The world says you are foolish to give to God, much less expect His blessing for doing so. God says to give a tithe to His storehouse and He will pour out a blessing on you. (See Mal. 3:10–11.)

The world says you are a fool to allow an enemy to get to you twice. God says to turn the other cheek when your enemy strikes you, giving him the opportunity to strike you again. (See Matt. 5:39.)

The world says that everything is relative and that truth is subject to conditions and interpretation. God says that His Word is absolute and unchanging. (See Mal. 3:6; Heb. 13:8.)

We must recognize that most of the world is moving in the wrong direction. Jesus taught, "Enter by the narrow gate; for wide is the gate and broad is the way that leads to destruction, and there are many who go in by it. Because narrow is the gate and difficult is the way which leads to life, and there are few who find it" (Matt. 7:13–14).

- *Can you identify from your experiences and your understanding of the Scriptures still other examples of how the Word of God is 180 degrees the opposite of conventional human wisdom?*

____

____

When God speaks to you, He calls you to His way of thinking and seeing. In the New Testament, this mind-set or perspective is called the mind of Christ. Would Jesus do this? If not, don't do it.

What the Word Says	**What the Word Says to Me**
Let this mind be in you which was also in Christ Jesus (Phil. 2:5).	______________________
Peace I leave with you, My peace I give to you; not as the world gives do I give to you. Let not your heart be troubled, neither let it be afraid (John 14:27).	______________________
Serve the LORD! And if it seems evil to you to serve the LORD,	______________________

choose for yourselves this day whom you will serve, whether the gods which your fathers served that were on the other side of the River, or the gods of the Amorites, in whose land you dwell. But as for me and my house, we will serve the LORD (Josh. 24:14–15).

Consider this question:

- *How do you feel about the likelihood that God will challenge you to be, say, and do things that are in conflict with conventional human wisdom?*

Clash with Fleshly Lusts

If what we hear urges us to gratify the flesh, without any thought to the consequences that are borne in the spirit or that affect our relationships with others, we should recognize immediately that what we have heard is not of God. God gives us messages that please the Spirit of God within us, not our lusts and sinful desires.

The Scriptures teach that every person must battle to some degree these kinds of self-gratifying lusts.

- The "lust of the flesh"—human appetites and sexual desires that are not in keeping with God's plan for marriage.
- The "lust of the eyes"—covetousness and greed for material goods.

- The "pride of life"—the desire for power and status that exalt one over others. (See 1 John 2:16.)

We err when we dismiss these lusts as irrelevant to us as Christians. We overcome lusts and temptations by the power of the Holy Spirit, but we never become immune to human appetites, a desire for goods and wealth, or a longing for fame, power, or prestige.

We are self-centered creatures and whether we want it to be so or not, we are usually out for number one (ourselves). We must keep in mind that God's voice does not feed our self-centered natures, but He calls us to righteousness, purity, and an unselfish giving of ourselves to others.

What the Word Says	What the Word Says to Me
Do not love the world or the things in the world. If anyone loves the world, the love of the Father is not in him. For all that is in the world—the lust of the flesh, the lust of the eyes, and the pride of life—is not of the Father but is of the world (1 John 2:15–16).	____________________ ____________________ ____________________ ____________________ ____________________ ____________________ ____________________ ____________________ ____________________
Seek first the kingdom of God and His righteousness, and all these things shall be added to you (Matt. 6:33).	____________________ ____________________ ____________________ ____________________
Whatever things are true . . . noble . . . just . . . pure . . . lovely . . . of good report, if there is any virtue and if there is anything	____________________ ____________________ ____________________ ____________________

praiseworthy—meditate on these things (Phil. 4:8). _____________________ _____________________

Challenge to Grow in Faith

While a "measure of faith" has been given to every person, our faith is to grow. (See Rom. 12:3.) God desires that we come to the point where we have great faith.

When the disciples awoke Jesus to still the storm on the Sea of Galilee, He responded to them, "Why are you so fearful? How is it that you have no faith?" (Mark 4:40). In other words, Jesus was asking, "How is that you haven't used any of your faith in this situation?" He said to Peter after Peter walked on the water and then started to sink, "O you of little faith, why did you doubt?" (Matt. 14:31). Jesus clearly expected His followers to have faith, to use it, and to grow in their faith.

We grow in faith when we hear from God, obey what He says to do, and then recognize and acknowledge God's faithfulness to His word in our lives. If we aren't hearing from God, it's virtually impossible for us to grow in faith. The same is true if we aren't obeying Him, and if we aren't looking for His fulfillment of His word in us.

We must recognize that a faith challenge requires consistency, endurance, perseverance, and watchfulness on our part. We must continue to stand in faith until we see come to pass the thing for which God challenged us to believe.

Jesus told a parable about a widow who went repeatedly to a judge for justice until he responded to her. Jesus, in pointing out that God was not like the callous judge, said, "And shall God not avenge His own elect who cry out day and night to Him, though He bears long with them? I tell you that He will avenge them speedily." Then Jesus said this about our tendency to give up too soon in matters that call for our faith to grow: "Nevertheless, when the Son of Man comes, will He really find faith on the earth?" (See Luke 18:1–8.) Persevere in your believing once you have heard God speak to you. Endure until you see the fulfillment of God's word.

Now, not every decision you make will necessarily call for great faith, but in making decisions in which you aren't sure if you are hearing from God, you are wise to ask, Does this challenge my faith?

What the Word Says	What the Word Says to Me
The disciples came to Jesus privately and said, "Why could we not cast it out?" So Jesus said to them, "Because of your unbelief; for assuredly, I say to you, if you have faith as a mustard seed, you will say to this mountain, 'Move from here to there,' and it will move; and nothing will be impossible for you" (Matt. 17:19–20).	______________________
Read Luke 18:1–8 and then Luke 18:9–14, which is a parable Jesus spoke to some who were putting their faith in their own good works rather than in God.	______________________
Behold the proud, His soul is not upright in him; But the just shall live by his faith (Hab. 2:4).	______________________

The Call to Have Courage

Finally, a message from God will likely call for you to have courage. If you are being asked to move against the tide of conventional human wisdom and act in contradiction to your fleshly nature, and if you are challenged in your faith, you are going to feel as though you are taking a risk in obeying God's message to you. Any time you take a risk for God's purposes, you are going to need courage.

Joshua knew this need for courage. The Lord challenged him with the mission of getting thousands upon thousands of grumbling Israelites across the Jordan River so they might claim the land of promise as their own. Prior to their crossing the river, the Lord exhorted Joshua three times to have courage:

> Be strong and of good courage, for to this people you shall divide as an inheritance the land which I swore to their fathers to give them (Josh. 1:6).

> Only be strong and very courageous, that you may observe to do according to all the law which Moses My servant commanded you; do not turn from it to the right hand or to the left, that you may prosper wherever you go (Josh. 1:7).

> Have I not commanded you? Be strong and of good courage; do not be afraid, nor be dismayed, for the LORD your God is with you wherever you go (Josh. 1:9).

Take a close look at these verses. In the first verse, the Lord reminded Joshua of the promised blessing that lay before him. As you stand in faith, believing God to be true to His Word, and you step out in obedience to His voice, keep in mind God's promises to you.

The second time the Lord admonished Joshua to have courage, He said, in essence, "Stay on track. Don't stray from My commandments and laws." As you obey the Lord, you must stay in the Word, stay in fellowship with other believers, stay in prayer, and continue to listen keenly for God's voice.

The third time, the Lord said to Joshua, "Don't let yourself get scared or discouraged. Remember that the Lord is with you." Fear and discouragement are subject to your will. You can command fear to leave you in the name of Jesus. The same goes for worry or feelings of frustration that you aren't seeing God's results as quickly as you would like. Remind yourself daily of what you heard God say, stay close to Him, and refuse to allow yourself to give in to fear or discouragement.

The good news is that the Lord doesn't expect us to have courage on our own. The Lord tells us that if we will have courage, He will strengthen our hearts. (See Ps. 31:24.)

When God speaks to us, the fulfillment of His plans hinges to some degree on whether we respond with confident, courageous spirits. His voice leads us not into timid discipleship but into bold witness.

What the Word Says	**What the Word Says to Me**
Wait on the LORD; Be of good courage, And He shall strengthen your heart (Ps. 27:14).	____________________ ____________________ ____________________ ____________________
Watch, stand fast in the faith, be brave, be strong. Let all that you do be done with love (1 Cor. 16:13).	____________________ ____________________ ____________________ ____________________
Let your conduct be worthy of the gospel of Christ, so that whether I come and see you or am absent, I may hear of your affairs, that you stand fast in one spirit, with one mind striving together for the faith of the gospel, and not in any way terrified by your adversaries (Phil. 1:27–28).	____________________ ____________________ ____________________ ____________________ ____________________ ____________________ ____________________ ____________________ ____________________
God has not given us a spirit of fear, but of power and of love and of a sound mind (2 Tim. 1:7).	____________________ ____________________ ____________________

Don't Hurry to a Conclusion

Nowhere in Scripture does God tell anyone to rush blindly into a decision. There may be times when we need to hear from God and act quickly, but God will never tell us to rush in without consulting Him about His timing. We often rush in because we have failed to ask God about timing. We assume that when the Lord tells us to do something, He means right now. That may not be the case. He may instruct you or prompt you to wait for further instructions, or wait until certain conditions are fulfilled.

Take time to make certain that you have truly heard from Him and that you have heard clearly and precisely. Above all, make sure that He is finished with all that He has to say to you on a point before you rush off to obey Him. His message may include instructions to you about whom to contact, where to go, and how to proceed. Make sure you have all the directions, assurances, insights, and details that He desires to give you.

You should subject the whole of God's message to the points discussed in this lesson. Is the directive in its entirety consistent with God's Word, representative of God's higher wisdom and not conventional norms, in contrast with fleshly lusts, a challenge to your faith, and a directive that requires action and courage?

Consider these questions:

- *What new insights have you gained about the characteristics of God's messages?*

  ____

  ____

- *Recall an instance in which you believe you heard God speak to you. In what ways was that message in keeping with the five characteristics we have discussed in this chapter?*

  ____

  ____

LESSON 7

How We Can Tell If the Voice Is God's and Not Satan's

People often ask me, "When I listen for God to speak after I pray, I sometimes seem to hear two voices. How do I know if I'm hearing from God or from Satan?"

This is a legitimate question because the enemy of our souls also attempts to speak to us. We know from Jesus' temptation experience in the wilderness that Satan will try many tricks to convince us to listen to him instead of to God. (See Matt. 4:1–11.) The apostle Peter warned us that the devil is always on the prowl, seeking to get in a roar that instills fear or confusion. (See 1 Peter 5:8.)

We must be on the alert continually to make certain that the voice we hear as we pray and listen for God's answer is, indeed, God's voice.

Jesus told His disciples that He must go to Jerusalem and suffer many things from the religious authorities there. Eventually, He would be killed, but He would be raised from death the third day. (See Matt. 16:21.) Peter took Jesus aside and privately said to Him, "Far be it from You, Lord; this shall not happen to You!" (16:22). As well intentioned as Peter may have thought he was, his words were not God's words—they were words that lined up with Satan's message. Jesus turned to Peter and rebuked him, saying, "Get behind Me, Satan! You are an offense to Me, for you are not mindful of the things of God, but the things of men" (16:23).

Peter, a follower of Jesus from virtually the beginning of Jesus' earthly ministry, was likened to the archenemy himself. We need to recognize that sometimes Satan's voice comes to us not in our thoughts and imaginations, but through the words of other people, some of whom may seem to be well intentioned or say they love us.

The Bible assures us that there is a way to tell Satan's voice from that of our Lord. I believe we will hear some distinct differences in the messages.

Satan Says . . .	**The Lord Jesus Says . . .**
Do your own thing; do what you want to do.	Consider the effects of your behavior on others. Live a selfless, self-giving life.
Live for the moment.	Live with an eye to eternity.
Don't concern yourself with what others say.	Receive godly counsel.
You're as mature as you ever need to be. You're a grown-up.	Continue to grow and mature and to become more and more like Jesus Christ.

Certainly, the outcome is different for us when we follow Satan's voice and message rather than the Lord's. Satan's path always leads to loss, destruction, and death. The Lord's way always leads to abundant life and eternal life. (See John 10:10.) Part of the difference in outcome is in the way we feel about our lives and actions:

- The result of following Satan's dictates is frustration, dismay, and worry.
- The result of following the Lord's message is a great inner peace.

As we take a look at each of these concepts in this lesson, keep in mind that no one is immune to hearing Satan's voice and being deceived by it. We never reach the place where we can say that we are fully immunized against Satan's assault on our minds.

Effects on Other People

God sees the beginning from the ending of time, and He also sees all people and the full impact of what we say and do on others—both those we know and who are close to us, and those we don't know. God will never ask us to exhibit harsh or crude behavior; He will never lead us to do anything that might hurt another person, emotionally, spiritually, or materially. God always works for the good of all His people, not just a few.

Satan, on the other hand, tells us what we want to hear. He tells us that we shouldn't worry about the rippling effects of our lives on others. He tells us that every person is an island unto himself or herself and that we should do whatever we please.

Had Abraham weighed the possible ramifications of his dealings with Hagar, no doubt he would have resisted Sarah's pleas to produce a child with her maid. (See Gen. 16—17; 21.)

Had David thought of the severity of God's discipline over the numbering of his subjects in Israel and Judah, he probably would have listened to Joab's advice to halt the project. (See 1 Chron. 21.)

If you feel the Lord is leading you in a particular direction, ask yourself, How will this affect people around me? Will anybody be hurt by what I am about to do or say? Will others be blessed? Is this blessing just for me? Who may benefit from what I am about to undertake? These questions help you weed out Satan's influence and hear the message God desires to convey.

What the Word Says	What the Word Says to Me
It is good neither to eat meat [offered to idols] nor drink wine nor do anything by which your brother stumbles or is offended or is made weak (Rom. 14:21).	
See that no one renders evil for evil to anyone, but always pursue what is good both for yourselves and for all (1 Thess. 5:15).	
Let them do good, that they be rich in good works, ready to give, willing to share, storing up for themselves a good foundation for the time to come, that they may lay hold on eternal life (1 Tim. 6:18–19).	

Consider this question:

- *In your experience, have there been times when you knew that you acted solely for your benefit and neglected to take into consideration the welfare of others? What was the result?*

God Is Never in a Hurry

Many references in Scripture mention the "fullness of time." God isn't in a hurry. He deals in eternal consequences, and He continually seeks the fulfillment of the full scope of His plan and purpose.

Satan always encourages us to act immediately because he knows if we back off and think long enough about most things, we'll reconsider. If we feel an overwhelming urge to act spontaneously and immediately, we're probably better off to pull in the reins. God is interested in having all the details in their proper places.

King Saul lost his throne because he acted hastily. Chosen by the Lord to be king over Israel, he was instructed by the prophet Samuel to wait at Gilgal for seven days. When Samuel hadn't arrived on the seventh day, Saul decided to take matters into his own hands. He prepared burnt offerings to invoke the Lord's favor. Sure enough, as soon as Saul had made the offerings, Samuel arrived. Saul offered lame excuses, but his rashness disqualified him from a long and peaceful reign. Getting ahead of God is a terrible mistake, and the consequences are always distasteful. (See 1 Sam. 10:8; 13:8–14.)

On the other hand, Nehemiah, cupbearer to the Persian king Artaxerxes, patiently waited for God's timing. He sought the Lord, with fasting and prayer, for four months until the king asked Nehemiah why his appearance was downcast. Nehemiah explained his concern over the devastation of Jerusalem, and within days, the king sent Nehemiah to Jerusalem with full authority and all the necessary supplies for a major rebuilding project. (See Neh. 1—2:9.)

It isn't easy to wait patiently before the Lord until you are sure that you have the fullness of His message to you. But how much more satisfying the results are when you know that you have heard God's entire message!

What the Word Says	**What the Word Says to Me**
My soul, wait silently for God	____________________
alone,	____________________

For my expectation is from Him (Ps. 62:5).

See how the farmer waits for the precious fruit of the earth, waiting patiently for it until it receives the early and latter rain. You also be patient (James 5:7–8).

For which of you, intending to build a tower, does not sit down first and count the cost, whether he has enough to finish it—lest, after he has laid the foundation, and is not able to finish, all who see it begin to mock him, saying, "This man began to build and was not able to finish" (Luke 14:28–30).

Consider this question:

- *In your experience, have there been times when you got ahead of God or you rushed ahead to do His will with unsatisfactory consequences?*

Taking Advantage of Wise Counsel

The book of Proverbs has a lot to say about the value of wise counsel. Proverbs 13:10 declares, "By pride comes nothing but strife, but with the well-advised is wisdom." Proverbs 20:5 states, "Counsel in the heart of man is like deep water, but a man of understanding will draw it out."

We are to seek godly counsel and to hear from people who truly love the Lord and who are firmly grounded in His Word. I never advocate that a person seek out so-called professional counseling just for the sake of getting somebody else's advice. The counseling may be more damaging than the problem the person had in the first place. When we seek counsel from others, we must seek out people who are knowledgeable in their field, but in addition to that, they must be

- counselors who have no ulterior motive over our lives.
- counselors who are eager to hear from God and are eager for us to hear from God.
- counselors who base their opinions on the Word of God and are eager for us to check their advice against the advice of the Bible.

If your counselor doesn't have these three traits, find a new counselor!

What the Word Says	**What the Word Says to Me**
Assemble yourselves and come;	______________________
Draw near together,	______________________
You who have escaped from the	______________________
nations.	______________________
They have no knowledge,	______________________
Who carry the wood of their	______________________
carved image,	______________________
And pray to a god that cannot save.	______________________
Tell and bring forth your case;	______________________
Yes, let them take counsel to-	______________________
gether.	______________________
Who has declared this from an-	______________________
cient time?	______________________
Who has told it from that time?	______________________

Have not I, the LORD?
And there is no other God besides Me,
A just God and a Savior;
There is none besides Me (Isa. 45:20–21).

You younger people, submit yourselves to your elders. Yes, all of you be submissive to one another, and be clothed with humility, for "God resists the proud, but gives grace to the humble." Therefore humble yourselves under the mighty hand of God, that He may exalt you in due time (1 Peter 5:5–6).

Do not be unwise, but understand what the will of the Lord is. . . . Be filled with the Spirit, speaking to one another in psalms and hymns and spiritual songs, singing and making melody in your heart to the Lord, giving thanks always for all things to God the Father in the name of our Lord Jesus Christ, submitting to one another in the fear of God (Eph. 5:17–21).

Continually Value Spiritual Growth

Rebellious teens often say to their elders, "Don't tell me what to do! I'm a grown-up, too!" That is the attitude of many people toward the voice of God. It is an attitude of pride, based on an assumption that we know as much about any given situation as God knows. Nothing could be farther from the truth.

Ultimately, God speaks to us in terms of our surrender to His desires. His messages to us aren't about what we want—which is usually limited, self-centered, narrow-minded, and shortsighted. Rather, His messages are about what He wants for us—which is always eternal and loving, and calls us to a higher and better way.

The Lord's messages are about our yielding to Him, our taking up the cross and following Him, our giving up our lives for others, our bearing one another's burdens, our encouraging one another and building up one another, our behaving in a way that causes others to walk in righteousness before the Lord.

Satan comes to us and tells us that we are wise enough in our own understanding to make decisions. This has been the temptation to humankind since the Garden of Eden—just eat of the fruit and you will be wise as gods. In our day, the lie may be, "Just do your research," or "Just get this degree," or "Just take this seminar," or "Just follow common sense." All of these may be good things to do, but we err if we put our trust solely in our own efforts and fail to get the wisdom of God. The result is just as disastrous for us as it was for Adam and Eve. We find ourselves in trouble anytime we assume that we can make decisions totally on our own.

What the Word Says	**What the Word Says to Me**
As newborn babes, desire the pure milk of the word, that you may grow thereby, if indeed you have tasted that the Lord is gracious (1 Peter 2:2–3).	______________________ ______________________ ______________________ ______________________ ______________________
We should no longer be children, tossed to and fro and carried about with every wind of doctrine, by the trickery of men, in	______________________ ______________________ ______________________ ______________________

the cunning craftiness of deceitful plotting, but, speaking the truth in love, may grow up in all things into Him who is the head—Christ (Eph. 4:14–15).

Beware lest you also fall from your own steadfastness, being led away with the error of the wicked; but grow in the grace and knowledge of our Lord and Savior Jesus Christ (2 Peter 3:17–18).

A Peace Beyond Understanding

The net result of hearing the voice of Satan is a gnawing, nagging feeling of frustration in your spirit. If you believe you have heard from God, and yet you continue to experience a feeling of uneasiness and questioning as you attempt to obey the voice you have heard, stop and take note. You have not heard from God!

God's voice brings about a deep calmness in the spirit. Although we may be challenged by what God says for us to do, we will not have a sense of inner conflict, worry, or a troubled heart.

The peace that God gives us is what the apostle Paul described as peace "which surpasses all understanding" (Phil. 4:7). This is peace that comes with a settled heart. This inner peace is not shaken, regardless of circumstances. When that sort of peace comes to us, we know we've heard from God, and we feel confident it is His voice: "Let the peace of God rule in your hearts" (Col. 3:15).

Some people have calloused consciences and don't seem to feel anything in the wake of a bad decision. Not feeling anything is a bad state to be in! After you have attempted to hear from God and have reached a decision about something in your life, you will feel one way or the other about it. Either you will have an abiding sense of calm, purpose, and peace, or you will feel uneasy, dissatisfied, out of sorts, frustrated, worried, or uncomfortable. Pay attention to this feeling that flows from your innermost being. It is a confirming sign to you that you have or have not heard from God.

Identifying His Voice

Over time, you will grow in your ability to discern whether the voice you are hearing is that of the Lord God. The same is true for the voice of any person with whom you have a relationship. As a child, I often heard my mother calling me to dinner. I didn't have to wonder for a split second whether the voice was that of my mother. I had grown up hearing it. A thousand mothers could have called my name, but I responded only to *my* mother's voice. As you develop an ear to hear what God is saying to you, you will come to know His voice unequivocally and immediately. He is your Father, and He calls you by name.

Consider this question:

- *How do you feel today about your ability to discern God's voice?*

  ____

  ____

LESSON 8

Our Predisposition to Hear

What you hear from God is determined in part by the attitude that you carry into any conversation with Him.

Our mind-set toward a conversation with God is affected by these things:

- Our prior relationship with God
- Our understanding about God
- Our attitude toward God

Anytime we go into a conversation with God, we go into that encounter with some history. We have an attitude toward God based on our understanding of Him. And the result is that we are predisposed to hearing certain things from God and not hearing other things.

Have you ever tried to tell something to someone and she didn't seem to understand you, no matter how many different ways you tried to tell her? It's as if she had a blockage of some kind or an aberration in her mental processing. That's the way it is with us in prayer. If we have no prior relationship with God, if we have a faulty understanding of Him, or if we have the wrong attitude toward Him, we aren't going to hear what the Lord wants to say to us. The fault is not His. It's ours!

You may have the feeling as you read through this lesson that you are being blamed in some way if you don't seem to be able to discern God's voice or hear from Him clearly. Blame is not at all the intention of this lesson. Rather, my hope is that you will recognize some of the blocks that may have been built into your spirit toward God—perhaps through faulty parenting, bad teaching, unexplained circumstances, or your rebellion. As you recognize these blocks, ask the Lord to dissolve them. Open yourself to His healing power. Ask Him to give you ears to hear.

Our History with God

Each of us has a history with God that began even before birth. God has ordained us to be on the earth, and He has a plan and a purpose for us, even though we may not have recognized them.

The only message that an unbeliever will hear from God, however, is that she is a sinner who needs to look to Jesus as Savior. Until a person has received Jesus Christ as his personal Savior, by faith, he will not be able to hear God speak on any subject other than salvation.

If you are having trouble hearing from God, you may need to reevaluate your relationship with Him. God is not motivated to speak to any of us on the basis of our good deeds or our needs. He is motivated to speak to us because He has a relationship with us.

When we receive Jesus Christ as our personal Savior, the Bible says we are born again. We are taken from the kingdom of darkness and placed into the kingdom of light. We become the children of God. Our salvation experience is the beginning of a two-way relationship with God.

Once we have accepted Jesus Christ as our Savior, we must take a second step. Salvation establishes relationship and settles the matter of our eternal security. But then we move on from salvation into identification with Jesus Christ. He becomes not only our

Savior but also our Lord. That is, Christ's life is now ours, and our lives are now His. As the apostle Paul taught, "It is no longer I who live, but Christ lives in me" (Gal. 2:20).

In identification, I take on the mind-set that what happened to Jesus happened to me. He was crucified at Calvary. My fleshly life was crucified, and my sins were nailed to the cross. Jesus was buried and raised. I was buried and raised to a newness of life that will be unending. Identification is the theme song of Romans 6.

When we accept, by faith, that sin's power over us has been broken by Jesus Christ, we are free to walk in the Spirit and to become the persons God wants us to be. We no longer live for ourselves and on our own. We continually seek to live as Jesus would live, and we trust Him to empower us and enable us to do so.

The extent to which we seek to identify with Jesus will determine, in part, what we hear God say to us. If we are content only with the fact that we are saved, then we probably aren't going to hear God speak to us about the ways in which He desires that we become more and more like Jesus. But if we are seeking continually to become more like Jesus, truly making Him the Lord of our lives, we are going to be listening for God's counsel about how we can be more like Him. He will speak to us readily about sins we need to confess, relationships we need to make right, new behaviors and opinions we need to adopt, new activities we need to pursue, and new blessings that are ours for the accepting.

Consider this question:

- *What is your relationship with the Lord Jesus Christ?*

  ____

  ____

What the Word Says	What the Word Says to Me
You are not in the flesh but in	------------------------
the Spirit, if indeed the Spirit of	------------------------
God dwells in you. Now if any-	------------------------

one does not have the Spirit of Christ, he is not His. . . . For as many as are led by the Spirit of God, these are sons of God (Rom. 8:9, 14).

I am the vine, you are the branches. He who abides in Me, and I in him, bears much fruit; for without Me you can do nothing. . . . By this My Father is glorified, that you bear much fruit; so you will be My disciples (John 15:5, 8).

In Him we live and move and have our being (Acts 17:28).

Our Understanding About God's Nature

What we hear is affected by our understanding of who God is. Each of us seems to be born with a mental grid system of opposites. As we grow and have experiences, we categorize them as good or bad, plus or minus, helpful or harmful. Over time, this grid system of opposites creates in us an overall perspective on life—some might call this our worldview or our mind-set. We transfer some of our thinking from the past into new areas of experience.

Below are seven opposite statements about your heavenly Father. Place a mark somewhere on the line to indicate the degree to which you tend to agree with each statement. Be honest with yourself!

God is . . .

Loving Father _ _ _ _ _ _ _ _ Demanding Father

Intimate Friend _ _ _ _ _ _ _ _ Distant Friend

Patient Teacher	_ _ _ _ _ _ _ _	Intolerant Teacher
Gentle Guide	_ _ _ _ _ _ _ _	Angry Guide
Understanding Counselor	_ _ _ _ _ _ _ _	Insensitive Counselor
Generous Provider	_ _ _ _ _ _ _ _	Reluctant Provider
Faithful Sustainer	_ _ _ _ _ _ _ _	Inconsistent Sustainer

Loving or Demanding Father?

Do you come before God expecting Him to accept you, love you unconditionally, and embrace you warmly? Or do you expect Him to ridicule you, put conditions on whether He will love you, reject you if you have erred, or fail on occasion to acknowledge you as His child? The Bible tells us that God's nature is love (1 John 4:8). Because of His love toward us, He sent His only begotten Son, that whoever believes on Him might have eternal life (John 3:16).

If you struggle in perceiving God as a loving God, look up all the verses in a concordance that relate to God's loving nature. Write them out. Memorize them. Develop a new grid system in your thinking about God's nature and His desires toward you.

Intimate or Distant Friend?

Do you come before the Father with freedom to say anything you like, trusting Him to understand you and not reject you? Or do you expect God to be like a bureaucrat who asks you to fill out your petitions in triplicate, take a seat in the corner, and wait until your turn is called as He considers your request? The Bible tells us that God is nearer than our breath. Jesus is a friend who "sticks closer than a brother" (Prov. 18:24). Jesus said to His followers that they were His friends, not His servants (John 15:15).

If you struggle to regard the Lord as an intimate Friend, read the Gospels and observe how closely Jesus lived in relationship with people who followed Him.

Patient or Intolerant Teacher?

Do you expect the Lord to teach you the error of your ways so you might improve, or do you expect Him to give you a letter grade of F, drop you from life's course, and suspend you from His school? God is not a critical Teacher who is always harping on your lack of spiritual understanding or continually waiting to punish you for each mistake or failure. He is a patient, kind, loving Teacher who woos you toward Himself and toward the way of righteousness.

If you think of God only as a Judge, and not as a patient Teacher, go again to the words of Jesus in the Gospels. Read what Jesus said. You'll find good reason for His followers to have called Him Rabbi—or Teacher.

Gentle or Angry Guide?

Do you see God as One who disciplines you so that you might get back on track or as One who punishes people in a fit of anger? Very often, people with abusive parents see God only as being harsh, unreasonable, and extreme in His discipline.

God gives us His rules and His chastisements to guide us in the way. Think for a moment what it would be like to be on a hike in a wilderness area with an experienced guide. You would likely do everything that guide asked you to do because you would see your very survival and return to civilization at stake. If you erred in your handling of certain gear, wandered away from the group, or took a wrong path, you would expect the guide to correct you quickly. You would follow his advice without question because you knew he was speaking for your benefit. The same is true for God as our Guide. He desires to keep us on His trail, using our resources and gear wisely, staying with other believers, so that we might ultimately come into the fullness of His kingdom.

Understanding or Insensitive Counselor?

Do you have a feeling when you come to God that He understands your concerns, or do you think of Him as either not knowing or not caring about your desires, temptations, issues, or emotions? Jesus came to show us that God does care about all aspects of our humanity. He is God's example that God understands how we feel and how difficult life can be, but He also knows that we can overcome temptations and live a pure and righteous life.

A good counselor attempts to help clients reach a place of greater health and wholeness. The Holy Spirit is just such a Counselor. He desires to bring us to wholeness, by binding up our wounds and giving us the inner strength to move forward in our lives.

If you struggle with the concept that God is an understanding Counselor, I encourage you to look up many of the references in a concordance that relate to *compassion, mercy,* or *merciful*. The Lord does understand, and He cares. As David wrote in Psalm 103:8, "The LORD is merciful and gracious, slow to anger, and abounding in mercy."

Generous or Reluctant Provider?

Do you see the Lord as delighting in you, generously pouring out on your life all the riches of His glory? Or do you see Him as a stingy God who plays favorites and withholds what you deserve, much less what you desire? The Scriptures tell us that God has infinite resources that He wants to give us. He clearly spells out how we can be in a position to receive them all! The most famous story in all the Bible, usually called the story of the prodigal son, should be called the story of the loving father, in my opinion. In this story, we see the portrait of a God who is ready and willing to bless His children with wonderful things. Luke 6:38 assures us that God causes blessings to come into our lives in "good measure, pressed down, shaken together, and running over."

If you struggle with the concept of God as a generous Provider, read again about how He provided for the Israelites in the wilderness and all of the verses that relate to giving and receiving. Our God is a generous God!

Faithful or Inconsistent Sustainer?

Do you come before the Lord with a knowing in your heart that He is trustworthy, reliable, and consistent? Or do you question whether God might be there for you in your hour of need?

The Bible proclaims from cover to cover that God is on our team. He never abandons us. We can count on Him. Lamentations 3:22–23 assures us,

> *His compassions fail not.*
> *They are new every morning;*
> *Great is Your faithfulness.*

If you struggle with the concept of God's faithfulness, look up the word *faithful, faithfulness,* or *lovingkindness* in a concordance, and read the references associated with the faithful, utterly consistent nature of God. God is the same, yesterday, today, and forever. His nature never changes. His desire for us is constant. His presence is abiding and eternal.

- *Having taken a look at your profile of how you understand the nature of God, do you see ways in which your thinking needs to be adjusted so that it is in alignment with God's Word?*

  ____

  ____

- *Do you have negative feelings about God? Focus on your feelings. Are you willing to let go of negative feelings and trust God? Are you willing to ask Him to help you approach Him with a new set of feelings?*

  ____

  ____

Our Attitude Toward God

We must have three overriding qualities in our attitude as we approach God.

1. We must be submissive. We must recognize that we are finite and He is infinite. We must recognize that we are created and He is the Creator. We must be willing to do what He says to do.

If we don't have this attitude toward hearing from God, we desire for God to put His stamp of approval on our preconceived ideas and plans, or we desire for God to tell us that we have done the right thing (which may not be the case). With that attitude, we cannot hear the fullness of what God desires to say to us. We need to recognize that our attitude is one of pride—that we are approaching God as if we are certain of our success and sure of our decision-making abilities.

2. *We must trust Him.* If we don't intend to trust God, we will never listen fully to all the details He will give us about how to obey Him. It's as if we are saying to God, "I'll hear what You have to say, but I don't believe You will be faithful to any of Your promises, trustworthy in helping me, or honest in Your appraisal." We must come before the Father absolutely convinced that God is going to lead us in the right direction and that He will enable us to be and to do all that He has challenged us to be and to do.

3. *We must come before Him with a thankful heart.* The Scriptures tell us that we are to enter His gates with thanksgiving. We come with an eye toward what God has done for us in the past. That puts us in a faith reception mode to receive what He has for us in the present and future. When we look back over our lives and recount all of the ways in which God has been good to us—and this is something we can do, regardless of how difficult our lives may have been—we must recognize that God is for us!

What the Word Says	**What the Word Says to Me**
Submit to God. Resist the devil and he will flee from you. Draw near to God and He will draw near to you. Cleanse your hands, you sinners; and purify your hearts, you double-minded. Lament and mourn and weep! . . . Humble yourselves in the sight of the Lord, and He will lift you up (James 4:7–10).	______________________
Trust in the LORD with all your heart, And lean not on your own understanding; In all your ways acknowledge	______________________

Him,
And He shall direct your paths
(Prov. 3:5–6).

Enter into His gates with thanks-
giving,
And into His courts with praise.
Be thankful to Him, and bless
His name.
For the LORD is good;
His mercy is everlasting,
And His truth endures to all gen-
erations (Ps. 100:4–5).

Consider these questions:

- *What new insights have you gained about what might be hindering you from hearing all that God has to say to you?*

- *In what ways do you feel challenged today as you attempt to listen to God with unstopped ears?*

LESSON 9

HOW TO LISTEN *ACTIVELY*

Samuel was one of the greatest prophets in the Old Testament. I don't believe it's a coincidence that his first assignment from God was to listen for God's voice:

> And the LORD called Samuel again the third time. So he arose and went to Eli, and said, "Here I am, for you did call me." Then Eli perceived that the LORD had called the boy. Therefore Eli said to Samuel, "Go, lie down; and it shall be, if He calls you, that you must say, 'Speak, LORD, for Your servant hears.'" So Samuel went and lay down in his place. Now the LORD came and stood and called as at other times, "Samuel! Samuel!" And Samuel answered, "Speak, for Your servant hears" (1 Sam. 3:8–10).

What a beautiful way to answer God, "Speak, for Your servant hears"! Eli taught Samuel how to listen to God. I don't believe there's a more important lesson that a parent can teach a child today.

This story of Samuel tells us that there is a difference between *active listening* and *passive hearing.* Hearing is something you do with your ears. If your hearing is normal, you can't help hearing sounds that are within a certain range and a certain spectrum of sound. Listening, however, involves the mind. And we all know that we can hear sounds without paying much attention to them. (Some people can sit in church and hear entire sermons without listening to them!)

Genuine listening is active. It involves putting the mind in gear to hear everything that is said as if it has meaning to the listener.

That's how God calls us to listen to Him—actively. He wants our full and undivided attention. There are ten key aspects to listening actively:

1. Expectantly
2. Quietly
3. Patiently
4. Confidently
5. Dependently
6. Openly
7. Attentively
8. Carefully
9. Submissively
10. Reverently

We'll go over each aspect briefly in this lesson. As you read about each one, I encourage you to think about your life. Ask about each step, Do I do this? Is this the way I open myself to receive God's message to me? I believe that you probably will feel a certain degree of conviction about one or more of these listening characteristics, since very few of us actively listen for God's word to us at all times. Consider that area of your perceived weakness or shortcoming to be an area for growth.

Listening Expectantly

If we are going to listen actively, we must come before the Lord expectantly. We must anticipate with eagerness His speaking to us. Throughout Scripture, we have the promise that God will speak to us. Jeremiah 33:3 records, "Call to Me, and I will answer you, and show you great and mighty things, which you do not know." Our expectancy is based on the Lord's reliability. What the Lord says, He does. If He says that He will answer, He will.

Our expectancy is also an indication of our faith. If we truly believe God's promises to us, trust in God's total provision for us, and rely on God's faithfulness as our heavenly Father, we will expect Him to speak to us and act on our behalf for our good. The stronger our faith, the greater our expectancy!

What the Word Says	What the Word Says to Me
Read 1 Kings 18:20–39 to see how Elijah expected God to answer.	______________________ ______________________ ______________________
I have called upon You, for You will hear me, O God; Incline Your ear to me, and hear my speech. Show Your marvelous lovingkindness by Your right hand, O You who save those who trust in You From those who rise up against them (Ps. 17:6–7).	______________________ ______________________ ______________________ ______________________ ______________________ ______________________ ______________________ ______________________ ______________________ ______________________

Listening Quietly

The Lord says to us, "Be still, and know that I am God" (Ps. 46:10). If we are to hear from God, we must be quiet and let Him do the talking. Too many of us think of prayer only as a time of rattling off a list of requests, then getting up and going about the busyness of our lives.

Quietness is essential to listening. If we are too busy to sit in silence in His presence, if we are preoccupied with thoughts or concerns about the day, if we have filled our minds all day long with carnal interference and aimless chatter, we are going to have difficulty truly listening to the still small voice of God.

You may find that late night or early morning is a time of solitude and quiet for you. A noonday walk in a park may be a time when you can quiet your soul before the Lord. Ask the Lord to reveal to you a time and place where you might turn off the cares and worries of the world a while and listen to Him.

What the Word Says

What the Word Says to Me

Read Matthew 13:3–9, 19–23. Think how your mind may be the field and how important quietness is to your receiving the good seed of God's Word into your life.

My soul, wait silently for God alone,
For my expectation is from Him (Ps. 62:5).

Let us know,
Let us pursue the knowledge of the LORD.
His going forth is established as the morning;
He will come to us like the rain,
Like the latter and former rain to the earth (Hos. 6:3).

Listening Patiently

The Lord does not tell us some things all at once or instantaneously. Sometimes He speaks part of His message to us at one time, part at another. Sometimes we hear a message from Him only after we have been waiting for a season of time.

We would like to be able to say, “Lord, here’s my order today. Please give me an answer before I get up off my knees. . . . You have thirty seconds.” But that isn’t how the Lord works. He is not at our beck and call. We are at His command.

Even though we may wait for God’s answer for what seems to be a long time, God has not forgotten us. He is very likely changing and preparing us to hear His message. Let that process happen in your life!

What the Word Says

Rest in the LORD, and wait patiently for Him (Ps. 37:7).

I wait for the LORD, my soul waits,
And in His word I do hope.
My soul waits for the Lord
More than those who watch for the morning—
Yes, more than those who watch for the morning
(Ps. 130:5–6).

And being assembled together with them, [Jesus] commanded them not to depart from Jerusalem, but to wait for the Promise of the Father. . . . When the Day of Pentecost had fully come, they were all with one accord in one place. And suddenly there came a sound from heaven, as of a rush-

What the Word Says to Me

ing mighty wind, and it filled the whole house where they were sitting. Then there appeared to them divided tongues, as of fire, and one sat upon each of them. And they were all filled with the Holy Spirit and began to speak with other tongues, as the Spirit gave them utterance (Acts 1:4; 2:1–4).	______________________

Listening Confidently

We must be confident as we listen to God that we will hear what we need to hear. It may not always be what we want to hear, but we can trust God to tell us what we need to know so that we can make decisions and change certain things in our lives for our ultimate good.

Sometimes I find that people listen for God but with their hands clenched. They are afraid of what God will tell them; in part, they are afraid that they won't be able to do what God tells them to do, or they won't be able to live up to God's expectations for them.

Would a good parent tell a child, "Here's what I want you to do," and then not provide the child with information about how to do it? Certainly not. Neither will the Lord tell us to live, move, or act in a certain way and then not give us full instructions and sufficient information so that we can carry out His directives. We must be confident that the Lord is never setting us up for failure. He sets us up for success—success in His eyes, success for all eternity!

What the Word Says	What the Word Says to Me
Commit your way to the LORD, Trust also in Him,	______________________

And He shall bring it to pass.
He shall bring forth your righteousness as the light,
And your justice as the noonday
(Ps. 37:5–6).

I can do all things through Christ who strengthens me (Phil. 4:13).

Listening Dependently

Have you ever heard the comment, "Do it as if your life depended upon it"? That's the way we are to listen because our lives depend upon our hearing.

Do you read your Bible as if it is the very food you need for your spiritual soul, and that without it, you will starve? Do you listen for God to tell you what to do, with the awareness that if He doesn't tell you what to do, you really have nothing to do? That was the position of the prophets in the Old Testament. That was the position of Jesus in the New Testament. That was the position of the apostles as they attempted to do what Jesus called them to do. That is the position we are to take today.

We must have no agenda other than His agenda. We must have no schedule other than His schedule.

What the Word Says | **What the Word Says to Me**

For what man knows the things of a man except the spirit of the man which is in him? Even so no one knows the things of God except the Spirit of God. Now we have received, not the spirit of the world, but the Spirit who is from God, that we might know the things that have been freely given to us by God (1 Cor. 2:11–12).

Then I called upon the name of the LORD:
"O LORD, I implore You, deliver my soul!"
Gracious is the LORD, and righteous;
Yes, our God is merciful.
The LORD preserves the simple;
I was brought low, and He saved me.
Return to your rest, O my soul,
For the LORD has dealt bountifully with you (Ps. 116:4–7).

Listening Openly

We must come to God with hearts and minds open to receive whatever He chooses to give us. To listen openly means to be willing to hear God correct us as well as comfort us, to hear Him convict us as well as assure us, to hear Him chastise us as well as praise us. If we come to the Lord willing to hear only words of prosperity, blessing, and comfort, we will not always hear what God has to say.

Unfortunately, the more unwilling we are to hear words of correction, the greater our need grows for correction. Come before the Lord humbly depending on the Holy Spirit to bring to your mind the areas of your life that need to be changed. Accept both the positive and the negative things the Lord says to you about yourself. Recognize that His words of correction are for your good, and that they are just as loving as His words of comfort.

The minute you say to the Lord, "I'll do anything *but* . . . ," or "I'll go anywhere *but there,*" you are no longer open. The minute you say to Him, "I trust You in every area of my life except in the area of my . . . ," you are no longer open. The minute you say, "I don't believe You would ever . . . ," you are no longer open.

Don't put limits on what God may say to you.

What the Word Says	What the Word Says to Me
All Scripture is given by inspiration of God, and is profitable for doctrine, for reproof, for correction, for instruction in righteousness, that the man of God may be complete, thoroughly equipped for every good work (2 Tim. 3:16).	________________________
Show me Your ways, O LORD; Teach me Your paths. Lead me in Your truth and teach me (Ps. 25:4–5).	________________________

Listening Attentively

When I am preaching, I can always look out at the congregation before me and tell the people who are attentively listening for the Lord to speak to them personally. They often have a notepad open and a pen poised to take notes. They are diligently looking for God's directives.

To be attentive means literally to attend, or to pay attention, to each word. This is more than expectancy that God is speaking. It is listening to each word for all nuances of meaning, all aspects of the message God is giving. When we truly listen attentively, we don't miss a thing!

What the Word Says	What the Word Says to Me
Be watchful in all things (2 Tim. 4:5).	____________________ ____________________
Be serious and watchful in your prayers (1 Peter 4:7).	____________________ ____________________
Every purpose of the LORD shall be performed (Jer. 51:29).	____________________ ____________________

Listening Carefully

To listen carefully means to listen for the Holy Spirit continually to confirm that the word we are hearing is a genuine word from God. We must put to that test everything we hear. It must line up with the written Word of God. It must be in keeping with the full example of the life of Christ. It must be in harmony with the way God has spoken to His people through the ages. To listen with care means that we care enough to evaluate every message we hear against the fullness of God's truth.

What the Word Says	What the Word Says to Me
Examine yourselves as to whether you are in the faith. Test yourselves (2 Cor. 13:5).	____________________ ____________________ ____________________
I have no greater joy than to hear that my children walk in truth (3 John 4).	____________________ ____________________ ____________________
A man's heart plans his way, But the LORD directs his steps (Prov. 16:9).	____________________ ____________________ ____________________

Listening Submissively

To listen submissively means that you listen with the full intent of obeying. If you plan to obey what you hear, you obviously take care to understand how the Lord wants you to do something—the attitude you should have as you live out His command to you—and with whom you should work. The Lord rarely calls us to undertake projects totally on our own. Even when the Lord calls us to reevaluate a certain aspect of our personal lives, He often directs us toward a person we can trust to be a wise counselor to us.

When Jesus went to the Garden of Gethsemane, He was already committed to the Father's will. However, He struggled with the Father to determine whether there was another way to accomplish God's purpose. There will be times when we come to God, listen to Him, and then grapple with what we hear. We may not be disobedient, but we may not understand how or why God is working in a certain way.

Being submissive does not mean that you automatically lose all your other longings or desires. They may be with you all your life. But in the end, submitting to God's word to you is the only way you will ever find genuine meaning and purpose in life.

Only as you submit to God are you in the precise position to hear from Him clearly and to be in a position where the Lord can do for you all that He has promised to do. As long as you have a mind of your own, you cannot fully have the mind of Christ. Don't let a spirit of rebellion impair your ability to listen.

What the Word Says	**What the Word Says to Me**
Every word of God is pure;	____________________
He is a shield to those who put	____________________
their trust in Him.	____________________
Do not add to His words,	____________________
Lest He rebuke you, and you be	____________________
found a liar (Prov. 30:5–6).	____________________

Read Luke 1:26–38—Mary's submission. ______________________

Read Matthew 26:36–42—Jesus' submission. ______________________

Listening Reverently

A reverent heart stands in awe of God. What a privilege we have to hear from the God of the universe, the Creator of all that is—seen and unseen—the almighty King, the all-powerful, all-knowing, eternal, loving Father. When we listen reverently, we listen with wonder—first, that God would speak to us, and then, that God would invite us to be a part of His plans and purposes.

You must never take God for granted. That is, you must never assume that God exists for your pleasure and bidding. Rather, you exist to worship, serve, and be a friend to God. He is the Lord. You are His follower.

What the Word Says	What the Word Says to Me
All the ends of the world Shall remember and turn to the LORD, And all the families of the nations Shall worship before You. For the kingdom is the LORD's, And He rules over the nations (Ps. 22:27–28).	______________________
At the name of Jesus every knee should bow, of those in heaven, and of those on earth, and of those under the earth, and . . . every tongue should confess that	______________________

Jesus Christ is Lord, to the glory of God the Father (Phil. 2:10–11). ______________________

Great is the LORD, and greatly to be praised (Ps. 48:1). ______________________

Listening with Ears to Hear

All of these aspects of active listening are ways in which we truly have "ears to hear." Jesus said repeatedly to His disciples, "He who has ears to hear, let him hear!" (See Matt. 11:15; 13:9, 43.)

Active listening requires that you make these declarations in the inner spirit by faith as you listen to God:

1. I'm eager to hear what You are going to say to me (expectant).
2. I'm listening, Lord (quiet).
3. I'll wait until I hear from You (patient).
4. I'm confident that You are going to tell me what I need to hear (confident).
5. I depend upon You completely to tell me who I am to become, what I am to say, and what I am to do (dependent).
6. I want to be open to all possibilities, Lord (open).
7. I am listening keenly to every word (attentive).
8. I am trusting You, Holy Spirit, to confirm to me that what I am hearing is, indeed, from God (careful).
9. Not my will or way, but Yours, Lord (submissive).
10. I am in awe and thanksgiving that You would speak to me, Lord (reverent).

When you truly listen actively, you can expect to hear from God in ways that compel you to action!

Consider these questions:

- *Are you an active listener? Rate your manifestation of active-listening traits:*

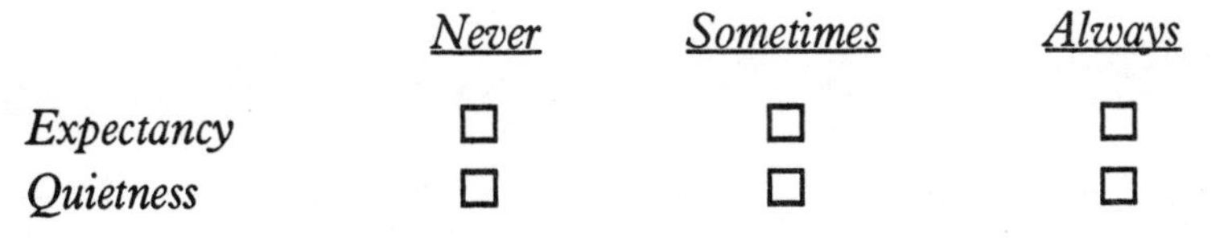

	Never	*Sometimes*	*Always*
Expectancy	☐	☐	☐
Quietness	☐	☐	☐

Patience	☐	☐	☐
Confidence	☐	☐	☐
Dependence	☐	☐	☐
Openness	☐	☐	☐
Attentiveness	☐	☐	☐
Carefulness	☐	☐	☐
Submissiveness	☐	☐	☐
Reverence	☐	☐	☐

- *How do you feel when you are listening actively, as opposed to hearing passively?*

  ____

  ____

- *What new insights have you gained about how to listen to God?*

  ____

  ____

LESSON 10

SITTING IN GOD'S PRESENCE

In this final lesson we want to put together many of the concepts we have covered in earlier lessons and go through a time of hearing from God in a step-by-step way.

This process is meditation. Meditation in recent years has been associated largely with Eastern religions, but we need to remember that Christians have practiced godly Bible-centered meditation for centuries. You may be more comfortable using the term *reflection* or *contemplation*. I like the phrase "sitting before the Lord."

When King David began making plans to build a temple for the Lord in Jerusalem, the Bible records that he "went in and sat before the LORD" (2 Sam. 7:18). That is a very descriptive phrase to me—one that defines our spiritual demeanor more than our physical posture. The usual position for Jewish prayer through the centuries has been to stand in God's presence. David was sitting, kneeling and resting back on his heels, humbly listening for what God was going to say to him.

There are five basic steps in this process:

1. Setting aside time
2. Getting still before the Lord
3. Recalling the Lord's goodness
4. Making a request
5. Submitting the will to God's answer

As we discuss each step, I encourage you to think, *How can I do this?* It isn't enough to learn these steps. You need to do them and have an experience of listening to and hearing from God.

After we have gone through the steps of meditation, we'll turn to the results that virtually all people experience after a time of meditation:

1. A deep, abiding sense of inner peace
2. A renewal of a positive attitude
3. A feeling of personal intimacy with the Lord
4. An inner realization of purification
5. A passion to obey

If you truly approach your prayer and Bible-reading time as sitting in God's presence,

- *How do you usually feel after spending time in prayer and reading God's Word? What would you like to feel?*

  ____

  ____

Setting Aside Time with God

Meditation requires a commitment of time. I encourage you to think of this as a season of time. The exact length of time, whether five minutes or an hour, will be determined largely by your purpose and your state of being as you come before the Lord. If you are in deep distress or if you face a major decision in your life, you should count on spending a longer time with the Lord.

Discuss your need to be alone with the Lord with your family members and others who depend on you. Find a time and place where you can be exclusively with Him. Make an appointment with the Lord. I sometimes go away for a weekend or an entire week to be alone with God. At other times, I designate a half day to do nothing but sit in God's presence with my Bible open before me. Set aside enough time to go through the process of slowing down. It takes a while for us to turn our full attention away from the cares of the world.

In anticipation of your time with the Lord, ask the Lord to do these three things in your life:

1. "Lord, let me have an open mind and heart." Don't come into a meditation time with a closed spirit.

2. "Lord, let me have a clear mind and heart." Your desire must be to hear the voice of God with certainty and to have a firm understanding that what you have heard is in line with the totality of God's Word. Ask the Lord to remove any doubt or vacillation from your thinking.

3. "Lord, let me have an uncluttered mind and heart." Ask the Lord to help you put aside the worries, frustrations, concerns, hurts, and the daily cares you have about relationships, business, school, work, money, food, shelter, and so forth. Ask the Lord to help you stay focused on Him during your meditation time.

Your goal in coming before the Lord is to have a committed mind to hearing from the Lord, not to have a closed, cloudy, or cluttered mind. Ask the Lord to help you in this regard so that your meditation time will bear much good fruit.

The feelings associated with setting aside time are usually eagerness, anticipation, focus, self-control, purpose, and a hunger to hear from God.

- *What are your feelings? (Record them after your time of meditation.)*

  ____

  ____

Getting Still Before God

As you begin your time of meditation, get still before God. Fix your thoughts on Him. True stillness before the Lord involves a sense of relaxation and of total ease in the Lord's presence.

I find that the most wonderful stillness I feel in God's presence is when I see Him as Friend, walking and talking with me along the beach or mountain trail, sitting beside me in an easy chair in my living room or study, sitting opposite me at the kitchen table. The Lord desires to be with you.

The feelings often associated with stillness are awe, wonder, awareness, closeness, ease, delight, and timelessness.

- *What are your feelings? (Record them after your time of meditation.)*

____

____

Recalling the Goodness of God

Many times in the Old Testament, the people of God were called to remember all the good things God did for them. As you spend time in stillness of heart before the Lord, call to your mind the goodness of God.

- Review your past. Think back over your life and recall the many times in which God has protected you, provided for you, blessed you, and cared for you.
- Reflect on the Lord Himself—His greatness, His grace, His goodness. You may find it helpful to recall some of the names of God in the Bible—Jehovah, Yahweh, Elohim, which point to the nature of God as being everlasting, infinite in power, absolute in faithfulness.
- Remember God's promises. His promises in the Word are for all of His children of every generation. He promises to provide for us and to work all things to our eternal good, to protect us from evil, to grant us His peace, to forgive us of sin when we turn to Him, to give us His Spirit, and never to leave or forsake us.

The feelings associated with this step of meditation are usually joy, faith, an outpouring of love, thanksgiving, humility, praise, a positive feeling about the future, and an eagerness to see what God will do next.

- *What are your feelings? (Record them after your time of meditation.)*

___

___

Making Your Request

So many of us rush to this phase. But how much more meaningful to make a petition to the Lord after we have entered into His presence with a committed mind and heart, having removed the hindrances of sin or false understanding about God that might keep us from hearing Him clearly. How different our requests are likely to be after we have spent time with the Lord recalling His work in our lives, His glorious nature, and His promises to us. We are far more likely to ask for the genuine desires of our hearts, not mere superficial wishes.

State your request in as simple terms as possible. Get to the very heart of what you want the Lord to do for you, in you, or through you.

The feelings often associated with making a request are humility, release, and freedom. When you make an appropriate request before the Lord, you have a sense that you are asking something the Lord desires for you. If you have to build a case for your request, you probably are asking in error.

- *What was your request? (Record it after your time of meditation.)*

___

___

- *Was your petition different from what you had anticipated before you entered your time of sitting in the Lord's presence?*

___

___

Submitting Your Will to God's Answer

As you make your request, be aware of any pride in your heart. Ask Him to remove pride from your heart.

Be aware of any unbelief that God can't or won't answer your request. Be aware of any answers that you are likely to reject out of hand even before God speaks. Ask Him to help you in your unbelief.

Pray again that the Lord will keep your mind open, unclouded, and uncluttered. Then, sit before the Lord and wait for His response to you.

The feeling one generally has at this point in meditation is a sense of giving up, surrendering, yielding, allowing, opening up, or receiving.

- *What are your feelings? (Record them after your time of meditation.)*

  ____

  ____

Gaining a New Perspective

When we meditate on the Lord, we see things from a different perspective. The things that have occupied our minds lose their grip. New things awaken in us. We feel stronger and better able to face life. Psalm 36:9 asserts, "In Your light we see light." There is something about God shedding His enlightenment on a subject that causes us to see clearly His truth.

The apostle Paul prayed that the Ephesians might be given a "spirit of wisdom and revelation in the knowledge of Him, the eyes of your understanding being enlightened" so that they might know the hope of His calling, the riches of the glory of His inheritance, and the exceeding greatness of His power toward them (Eph. 1:17–18).

What a wonderful thing to experience! If we truly come away from a time of sitting in the Lord's presence with renewed hope, an awareness of all that He has for us, and an assurance that He can and will act in power to bring about all that He has said, surely there is nothing that will seem impossible to us!

Very specifically, you can expect these five feelings to pervade your entire being as the result of a time spent in meditation before the Lord:

1. Peace. Jesus said, "My peace I give to you" (John 14:27). Christ's presence in you gives you a deep assurance and an abiding sense of rest. Your mind will no longer be tossed to and fro with wildly divergent ideas and opinions. Your heart will no longer feel troubled. Your spirit will no longer be agitated or feel pressed down under a heavy burden. You will know peace.

2. Positive attitude. This is not simply positive thinking. This is an all-encompassing attitude that God is in charge, and therefore, things are going to turn out according to His plan and purpose. A person with this attitude can't wait to get up the next day to see what God is going to do!

3. Personal intimacy. You have a feeling after a time of deep meditation with the Lord that you have shared yourself fully with Him, and that He has shared Himself fully with you. God is not detached, aloof, or far away. He is nearer than near. He is within you, and you are within Him.

4. Purification. A time of sitting with the Lord makes you feel clean inside. The Lord's presence is a purifying presence. The longer you are with Him, the more you see yourself for who you are, the more willing you are to face your sins and ask His forgiveness, the more He forgives, and the greater the cleansing you feel.

With purification comes a feeling of release, freedom, and eagerness to move forward with strength.

5. Passion to obey. You can come before the Lord tired in body, weary in spirit, emotionally distraught, fragmented in mind, and find that after a time of meditation with the Lord, you feel energy, power, strength, and renewed enthusiasm for life. God works from the inside out in refreshing you. And the result is that you have an eagerness to get up and get moving and actually do what the Lord has revealed to you as His desire for your life. You feel an eagerness—indeed, a zeal—for following the Lord and receiving all that He has prepared for you. You want to do His will and walk in His ways because you know that it will be not only for the glory of His name but also for your eternal benefit.

These five manifestations of renewal—peace, positive attitude, personal intimacy, purification, and passion to obey—confirm that you have spent time with God. His precise answer may not have been revealed to you during your meditation time, but you have the assurance that God has heard your petition and that His answer is on the way! You feel confident that as you continue to listen, you will hear all that He has to say to you.

If you spend time with the Lord and you don't experience these five manifestations in your life, I encourage you to spend more time with the Lord. Go back to the beginning and ask the Lord to reveal to you which step you may have missed or shortchanged in the meditation process. Sit again in the Lord's presence, and do this as often as necessary until you feel peace, have a positive attitude, sense a deep personal intimacy with the Lord, are aware of inner purification, and have a passion to obey His word to you.

- *How would you describe your time of meditation to a person who has never experienced a time of sitting in the Lord's presence?*

  ____

  ____

Taking Time to Meditate

Now is the time to do this! If you are doing this study alone, identify a time and place when you can shut yourself away with God to hear from Him. If you are doing this study in a group setting, discuss with others in your group how and when you intend to spend time sitting before the Lord.

Identify in your heart the issues that are of greatest concern to you. They are the petitions you are taking into your meditation time. Be aware that these petitions may change as the result of your reminding yourself about God's work in your life, reflecting on God's nature, or recalling God's promises.

And then enter into a time of deep fellowship with the Lord.

After you have done so, reflect on how you felt about that experience and what direction the Lord gave you for your life. You may want to make a note in your Bible or perhaps discuss it with your group. Be as specific as you can be in identifying your feelings and the insights you have had as a result of meditating before the Lord.

Consider these questions:

- *What new insights have you gained about how to listen to God?*

  ____

  ____

- *In what areas do you feel challenged to grow further in your understanding of God's voice or God's message to you?*

  ____

  ____

EPILOGUE

MY FINAL WORD TO YOU

When we fail to listen to God, we open ourselves up to hearing other voices, to being deceived. The number one deception is always the same: we can make it through life on our own. We may call this independence, but God calls it pride.

If we are operating out of pride, we make decisions that satisfy our fleshly desires—our desires for things, self-gratification, or power over others. We begin to use and abuse people and to damage or destroy things.

Pride also causes us to make excuses for our wrongs and get into self-justification. This downward spiral through deception to pride to lusts to self-justification carries us farther and farther away from God. We ultimately suffer consequences, none of which are pleasant. We hurt others, and they are hurt even more because of what becomes of us. And when all has been said and done, we have missed out on God's best for our lives.

The opposite, of course, is an upward spiral that occurs when we desire to hear from God and are open to all that He has to say to us. The more we develop our relationship with God, the more we realize that we utterly depend on Him for everything in our lives, and that He is utterly dependable to provide for us everything we need.

Our dependence on God leads us to see others in a new light—as fellow human beings who also depend on God for forgiveness, provision, growth, protection, and blessing. We have a greater regard for others, and we do our best to live in a loving, harmonious relationship with them. We desire to do things that will provide for them and bless them.

Our dependence on God leads us to seek an ever closer walk with Him. We do not grow into independence; rather, we grow into greater dependence. We develop an intimate relationship with the Lord so that we sense His presence always and hear His voice virtually continually, directing us into His paths of righteousness. As we do this, we find ourselves filled to overflowing with His blessings. We experience God's best for us, which is beyond anything that we once might have thought or imagined. (See Eph. 3:20.)

Neither of these spirals is created in a day or in one time of meditation before the Lord. Each is a pattern that forms in our lives over time. Each is an indication of the overall direction in which we are moving—either away from God or toward God.

Listening to, and then obeying, God is the way to build a positive upward spiral in our lives. It is the primary way we grow in the Lord.

Are you moving in an upward spiral today? I trust that you are. And I pray that you will continue to move in an upward direction, becoming more and more like Jesus Christ every day of your life, until that day when you are taken to be with the Lord in the fullness of His glorious heaven, there to live forever.

Let me assure you of this: God is still speaking to you. He still has something more to say to you. Listen to Him today!

Books by Charles Stanley from Thomas Nelson Publishers

Eternal Security

The Gift of Forgiveness

The Glorious Journey

How to Handle Adversity

How to Keep Your Kids on Your Team

How to Listen to God

The In Touch Study Series
- *Listening to God*
- *Advancing Through Adversity*
- *Experiencing Forgiveness*
- *Relying on the Holy Spirit*

The Source of My Strength

Winning the War Within

The Wonderful Spirit-Filled Life